W9-CSJ-439

Mountains

Catherine Chambers

Heinemann Library

Customer Service 888-454-2279

Visit our website at www.heinemannlibrary.com

Designed by David Oakley
Illustrations by Tokay Interactive
Originated by Dot Gradations
Printed in Hong Kong/China

06 05 04 03 02
10 9 8 7 6 5 4 3 2 1

Library of Congress Cataloging-in-Publication Data
Chambers, Catherine, 1954-
    Mountains / Catherine Chambers.
      p. cm. – (Mapping earthforms)
    Includes bibliographical references (p.) and index.
    Summary: Examines the world's mountains, discussing how they were formed, what organisms live there, and how they are used by humans.
    ISBN 1-57572-525-8 (lib. bdg.)   ISBN 1-4034-0035-0 (pbk. bdg.)
    1. Mountains—Juvenile literature. [1. Mountains.] I. Title.

GB512.C53 2000
508.3143—dc21   99-046852

Acknowledgments
The Publishers would like to thank the following for permission to reproduce photographs: Robert Harding Picture Library, pp. 4, 20; Survival Anglia/Konrad Wothe, p. 5; G. R. Roberts, pp. 6, 21, 25; South American Pictures, p. 10; Robert Harding Picture Library/S. Harris, p. 12; Anthony King, p. 13; Ecoscene/A. Brown; p. 15; Ardea/B. Gibbons, p. 17; Bruce Coleman Collection/J. Grande, pp. 18, 19; Oxford Scientific Films/K. Su, p. 23; Still Pictures/S. Noorani, p. 24; Popperfoto, p. 26; Oxford Scientific Films/D. and M. Plage, p. 27; Oxford Scientific Films/G. Merlen, p. 29.

Cover photograph reproduced with permission of Robert Harding Picture Library.

Every effort has been made to contact copyright holders of any material reproduced in this book. Any omissions will be rectified in subsequent printings if notice is given to the publisher.

Some words are shown in bold, **like this.** You can find out what they mean by looking in the glossary.

Contents

What Is a Mountain? 4

The Mountains of the World 6

How Are Mountains Formed? 8

Exploding Mountains 10

What Do Mountains Look Like? 12

A Great Mountain Range—The Rockies 14

Mountain Plants 16

Mountain Animals 18

People of the Mountains 20

A Way of Life—Tibet 22

Changing Mountains 24

Looking to the Future 26

Mountain Facts 28

Glossary 30

More Books to Read .31

Index 32

What is a Mountain?

A mountain is a huge, steep-sided rock formation that rises above the earth's surface. Some people think that to be called a real mountain, a hill has to rise at least 3,200 feet (1,000 meters) above sea level. Others believe that the exact height does not matter.

Many mountains occur in a long chain, or **range**. Each peak in the range is often described as a separate mountain. Mountains can lie under the oceans, rising from the sea bed. Some stick out above the ocean water. Some of the earth's highest mountains are completely underwater.

How are mountains formed?

Most mountains are made in one of three ways. One is when the **plates** of the earth's crust are pushed together or upward,

Ayer's Rock is a sandstone rock in central Australia. It is nearly 4 miles (6 kilometers) long and just over 1 mile (2 kilometers) wide. But it is only 1,141 feet (348 meters) high, so many people call it a rock, not a mountain. When the sun sets, the light turns the rock a rich red color. Ayer's Rock is a sacred place for the Aboriginal people of Australia. They call it Uluru.

making the surface rock crumple and fold. A second way is when areas of soft rock are worn away, leaving peaks or **plateaus** of harder rock sticking out. A third way is when **molten** rock from deep within the earth shoots through gaps in the earth's crust and cools into a volcanic mountain.

What do mountains look like?

Mountains give the world some of its most amazing scenery. Mountains have many different shapes, patterns, and colors. A very high mountain can be lush and green at its base, but rocky and covered with snow at its peak. We will discover more about the great variety of mountain landscapes.

Life on the mountains

Life on the mountains can be difficult, especially at higher levels. Many plants have **adapted** to the cold winds and poor soil. Animals have learned to survive in the thin air and thick snow. People have adapted, too. We will also find out what the future holds for life in the mountains.

Mountains often mark borders between countries. The Ural Mountains in this picture do not separate two countries, but they form the boundary between two continents and two very different cultures. To the west lies European Russia, and to the east lies Asian Russia.

The Mountains of the World

Where in the world?

Mountains are found all over the world, in many different environments. Occasionally, single peaks and **ridges** rise suddenly above flat ground. Some mountains are islands that seem to pop out of the sea. Many of these are underwater volcanoes.

Most mountains are part of a **range**. These ranges are often found on the edges of continents. Each one has a cluster of peaks and ridges that were all formed at the same time and in a similar way. Ranges are often separated by a high, flat **plateau**.

Groups of ranges are called a mountain system or chain. Bigger groups are known as a **belt**, or **cordillera**. The biggest belts on land are the Himalayas in central Asia, the Rockies in North America, and the Andes in South America. Longer belts can be found in the sea.

The Great Dividing Range stretches down eastern Australia. It causes rain brought by constant winds to fall on the east side. To the west lies the Great Australian Desert.

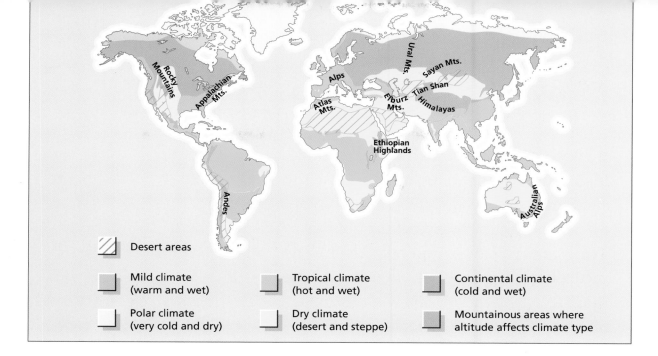

Desert areas

Mild climate
(warm and wet)

Tropical climate
(hot and wet)

Continental climate
(cold and wet)

Polar climate
(very cold and dry)

Dry climate
(desert and steppe)

Mountainous areas where
altitude affects climate type

Mountains and climates

Mountains are found in all types of **climates**, from the frozen lands of Alaska to the hot deserts of the Sahara. But mountains themselves can have a big effect on weather. The arrows on the map above show the direction of the main, constant winds. These winds blow rain clouds on to continents.

When the clouds meet mountain ranges, they rise and shed their rain. But the rain rarely reaches the other side. This is why so many deserts lie on one side of a mountain range. The deserts are in rainshadow areas. Mountains shape the weather around them, too. Ranges make their own small climate zones, which affect the plants, animals, and people that live on the slopes.

 Some winds blow in one direction nearly all the time. Mountain ranges keep the rain from going further. The deserts lie in the rainshadow areas on the other side of the mountains.

How are Mountains Formed?

The moving earth

Most mountains are formed because the earth moves. The continents rest on huge pieces of the earth's crust, called **plates**. The plates move around on a layer of hot, **molten** rock. This layer is known as the **mantle**. Many mountains were formed millions of years ago, when the plates bumped together or slid apart. Mountains are still slowly rising and changing shape as the plates continue to shift. This plate movement is called **continental drift**.

This map shows the earth's moving plates. It also shows active volcanoes. Many of these volcanoes form mountains where the plates meet. There are also many earthquakes in these areas.

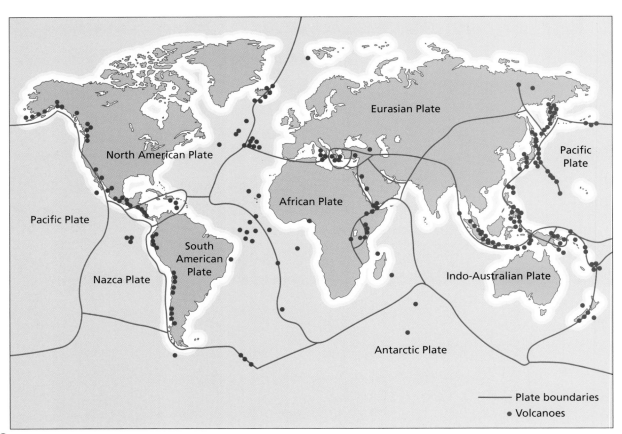

Eurasian Plate

North American Plate

Pacific Plate

Pacific Plate

African Plate

South American Plate

Nazca Plate

Indo-Australian Plate

Antarctic Plate

—— Plate boundaries
• Volcanoes

8

Fold mountains

Long ago, the plates jostled together and pushed the earth's crust upward. This crumpled the edges of continents and formed huge mountain **ranges,** such as the Himalayas and the Rockies.

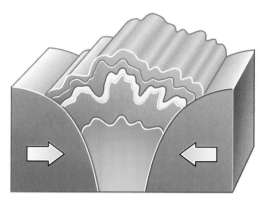

Fold Mountains

Block mountains

Movement under the earth's crust also makes cracks, called **faults,** in the rock. Blocks of rock slip up and down the faults, making some blocks rise above the others. These are known as block mountains. The Sierra Nevada range in the western United States is caused by faults.

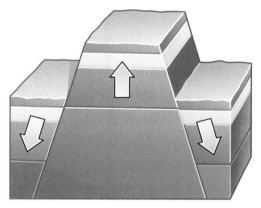

Block Mountains

Dome mountains

Dome-shaped mountains are formed when the earth's movements push up hot, melted rock called **magma** from under the ground. If the rock on the surface is too hard to crack open, the pressure causes a dome shape. The Black Hills of South Dakota are dome mountains.

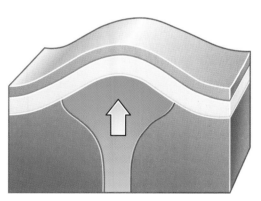

Dome Mountains

Worn mountains

Some mountains are made when soft rock is worn away by wind, rain, rivers, and **glaciers.** Harder rock above the softer rock of the **valleys** and **plateaus** remains. The Ozark Mountains in the southern United States were formed this way.

Exploding Mountains

Liquid mountains

Volcanic mountains occur where the earth's crust is thin and weak. Volcanoes can occur on land or under the ocean, where they often rise above the water as islands. Volcanoes often begin with hot gases, ash, and rocks exploding through cracks in the earth's surface, called vents. Hot **magma** rises from great chambers under the earth's crust and then oozes out through the vent. When magma reaches the air, it cools and becomes **lava**, which is thicker than magma.

The lava piles up and cools further into a cone-shaped volcano with a hole at the top called a **crater**. Sometimes lava spreads out over a wider area, making a shield-shaped volcano with gently sloping sides.

Mauna Loa is a shield volcano. It lies on the main island of Hawaii in the Pacific Ocean. The tallest mountain in the world is also a shield volcano. It is Mauna Kea, which lies on the same Hawaiian island. Only 13,792 feet (4,205 meters) of Mauna Kea is above sea level.

Some volcanoes grow into mountains very quickly, such as Mount Paricutin in Mexico. The land where it stands was a cornfield until one day in 1943 when smoke, ash, and volcanic rocks suddenly spurted out of a crack in the ground. Then burning orange lava gushed out. In one week it was a hill 490 feet (150 meters) high. Fifty years later it was 9,100 feet (2775 meters) high.

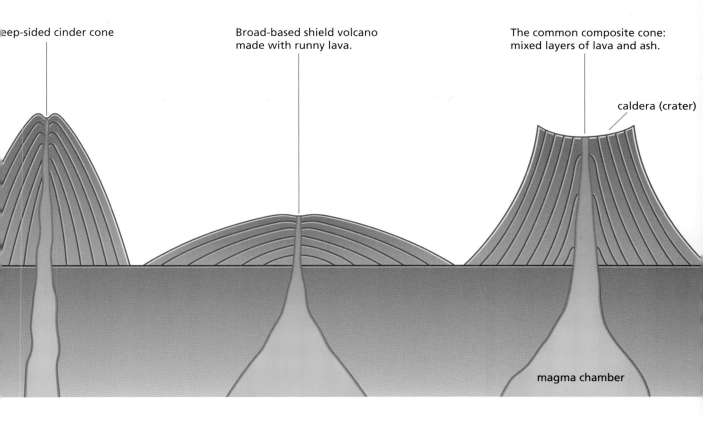

eep-sided cinder cone

Broad-based shield volcano made with runny lava.

The common composite cone: mixed layers of lava and ash.

caldera (crater)

magma chamber

Sleeping volcanoes

When a volcano has not erupted for millions of years, it is called extinct, or dead. But a volcano that has not erupted for thousands of years is still thought to be alive. It is called dormant, which means it is sleeping. Dormant volcanoes are very dangerous. Most have a **plug** of old, solid lava filling the crater. When the volcano finally explodes again, enormous pressure builds up against the plug. This leads to a huge eruption. Mount St. Helens in Washington was dormant for 123 years. But in 1980, magma pushed up against the solid rock. The pressure blew out a whole side of the mountain.

Volcanoes get worn down, just like any other mountain. When the soft layers of rock are **eroded** away, they leave a plug of hard, solid lava. Solid lava is often rich in **minerals**, which can make volcanic soils very **fertile.** This is why farmers are attracted to the slopes of volcanoes. Some volcanic craters fill with water and become lakes.

What Do Mountains Look Like?

Mountains can have jagged peaks or flat tops. They can be a single color or have bands of different colored rock. How a mountain looks depends on its age, the kind of rock it is made of, and how it has **eroded**.

Young mountain **ranges** have tall peaks and deep **valleys**, like the Alps in Europe. This is because erosion has not yet flattened them. Older mountains have rounder peaks and shallower valleys. The Appalachians in North America are like this.

Sun, rain, frost, and snow all wear down rocks. This is known as **weathering**. Rivers and **glaciers** carry away pieces of broken rock. These bump against the mountain,

Erosion can reveal patterned layers of different types of rock, as in the Grand Canyon in Arizona. **Igneous** rocks are made of hardened **magma**. **Sedimentary** rocks are made of bits of clay and gritty sand that were deposited by running water. **Metamorphic** rocks are smooth, such as marble, and have been heated and pressed. But not all mountains are made of layers. Some are made of just one type of rock.

wearing it away even more. This kind of erosion is known as **corrasion**. The most powerful erosive force is a river. It can cut deep **gorges** between the mountains. Frost shatters rocks into lots of jagged pieces called **scree**. These pieces are pulled down the mountain by gravity.

This beautiful formation is called the Enchanted City. It is made of limestone rock that has been eroded into fantastic shapes. The Enchanted City is in Spain's Sierra de Valdecabras.

Mountains are not just bare rock. Streams, waterfalls, and small rivers run down them. Glaciers slip slowly toward the bottom. Small lakes fill dips that were **scoured** out by glaciers. Mountain peaks are often covered in snow, and snowsheets cover flat slopes. Lower down, plant life colors the mountain green, except where the **climate** is very dry. Then, bare rock reaches to the valley floor.

Weather on the mountains

There are often clouds, rain, and snow on mountains. Warm clouds rise when they are blown up against the mountain. As the clouds rise, they cool in the chilly mountain air. This makes the **water vapor** in them turn into water droplets that fall as rain high on the mountain. The cold air also makes some of the rain fall as snow. On the other side of the mountain, the cold air sinks quickly. This can cause very strong air **currents**. These and other unusual weather features affect mountain life.

13

A Great Mountain Range— The Rockies

The Rocky Mountains, or Rockies, are a long **belt** of mountain **ranges** stretching along the western side of North America. These mountains were first folded upward more than 190 million years ago. They are still forming and rising. The chain has many different landscapes, from the peaks of Wyoming to the flat-topped rocks of the Grand Canyon. Most of the **erosion** has been caused by moving ice and water. The Rockies have wide **valleys scoured** out by **glaciers,** as well as deep **gorges** carved by rivers. There are long ribbon-shaped lakes

The Rocky Mountains make a **watershed** between different river systems. For example, the Colorado River flows westward from the Rockies into the Pacific Ocean. The waters of the mighty Missouri run eastward to the Mississippi River and eventually flow into the Gulf of Mexico, which opens out into the Atlantic Ocean.

14

and hot volcanic springs. The Great Salt Lake sits in the middle of the Rockies' widest point. The salt in the water comes from the **minerals** in the rocks around it.

The chain passes through many different **climates**, from the frozen lands of Alaska in the north to hot, sunny Mexico in the south. The Rockies also affect the climate to the west. They keep rain from reaching it, making it into a dry rainshadow area. Many rivers begin high in the Rockies, which form a division, or watershed, between different river systems.

Life in the Rockies

Very small plants grow on most of the Rockies' peaks. Further down are grasses and small shrubs. Below this lie huge forests, mainly of **conifer** trees, with grassland sloping away from them. The vegetation makes a good **habitat** for many different **species** of plants and animals.

About five million people live in the Rockies. Some people work in the mining industry. Gold, silver, copper, coal, and iron ore are found in the mountains. There is also oil and natural gas. Some people work in the forests, especially in the north. In the Colorado, Montana, and Wyoming Rockies, farmers raise large herds of cattle and sheep. Tourism also provides jobs. The Rockies have many popular ski resorts.

Rocky Mountain National Park was created in 1915. It includes many peaks, 60 of which are more than 11,480 feet (3,500 meters) high. Tourists can cross the park from east to west along Trail Ridge Road, which takes them over the Continental Divide. Deer, black bear, Rocky Mountain Bighorn sheep, elk, and coyote roam the park. Golden eagles fly overhead. The park is home to over 700 species of plants.

Mountain Plants

Growing problems

The diagram below shows different kinds of plant life in different mountain **climates**. But all mountain plants face many of the same problems. As the slope rises, the temperature cools. For every 500 feet (150 meters) of **altitude**, the temperature drops about 2° F (1° C). Plants also have to cope with rapid temperature changes, from very cold at night to hot during the day.

Mountain soils are thin and poor. Heavy rain makes any soil very wet. The soil often freezes, too. Strong winds blow, and clouds often block the sunlight that plants need for food and energy.

Mountains in the far north or south are only able to support vegetation on their lower slopes.

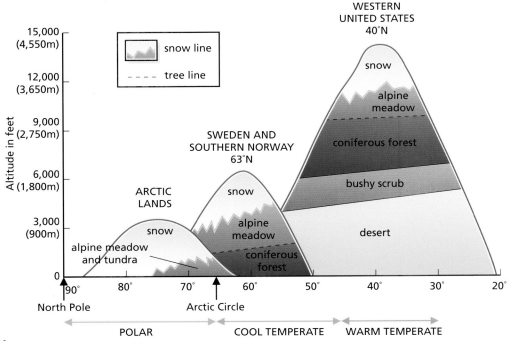

Tough plants

Mountain plants have **adapted** to the harsh conditions. High up, tiny **lichens** cling to bare rocks. Lichens are not true plants. They are a mixture of **fungi** and **algae**. Lichens are very tough and leathery. They do not need soil. Mosses are true plants, but they are also very tiny. They, too, cling and grow well in very damp conditions.

Lower down, larger plants often grow in sheltered cracks between the rocks. They flower and produce seeds in a very short time before the long, harsh winters begin. Most mountain plants have very strong, clinging roots and short stems that cannot break in the wind. Their leaves are small, flat, and covered in hairs, spikes, or spines. These leaves let in warmth and light, but are not harmed by wind and ice. The flowers are surrounded by leaves for protection. Grasses have a tough, waxy coating and are often bunched together like a bush. They sway in a rotating motion so that they do not snap when the wind blows.

Mountains often have an area of **conifer** trees. Most conifer trees are evergreen, which means that they do not lose their leaves during the winter. This enables them to use winter's weak rays of sunlight to make food. The leaves are thin and often spiky with a waxy coating. This keeps them from drying out when the tree roots are unable to get moisture from the frozen soil.

The silver fir grows in mountain forests throughout Europe, from the Pyrenees to the Alps and eastward to the Balkan Mountains. Its wood is used for making boxes and carvings. It is also made into paper. Turpentine oil is extracted from the bark and mixed into paints. Turpentine from the leaves and wood is used in medicine for both people and animals.

17

Mountain Animals

Mountain animals have to survive in very harsh conditions, just as the plants do. There is less oxygen for animals to breathe high in the mountains. This is because oxygen is a heavy gas that sinks. But many mountain mammals have developed large lungs and hearts to make the most of the small amount of oxygen available.

Many mammals live above the **tree line**. In the winter, some move from the peaks down to the **foothills**. Small mammals, such as alpine marmots, eat as much as they can during the summer. They store fat in their bodies and then **hibernate** in winter. The marmot hibernates in deep burrows that it fills with hay.

Mountain birds are usually large and strong, like this golden eagle. The golden eagle lives in Europe, Asia, Africa, and North America. It has to fly in very fierce winds. Golden eagles can grow up to 3 feet (1 meter) long from beak to tail, with a wingspan of 6 feet (2 meters). The eagle has very sharp eyes that help it spot its prey from very high up. Its strong talons grip small mammals to carry them away. The eagle eats meat ranging from mice to young deer. Its nest is made from sticks and twigs and is built high on rocky mountain ledges.

Many mammals have **adapted** to the cold temperatures. Large mammals, such as the yak, llama, and vicuna, often have thick, long fur. These shaggy coats trap the air warmed by the animals' bodies and keep them warm. The thick fur also protects them from the chill of the wind.

Many mammals are darkly colored. This helps them absorb the sun's warmth. Pale colors reflect more of the sun's heat and would make the animal colder. But others, such as the Arctic hare and Arctic fox, turn white in winter as **camouflage** against the snow. A white coat protects the hare from being caught by predators. It keeps the Arctic fox from being seen by its prey.

Mountain sheep, goats, and small mammals feed mostly on tough grasses and small shrubs. They can also eat **lichens** and mosses that cling to the rocks. The sheep and goats are able to climb on high, narrow ledges to find their food. The Rocky Mountain goat has soft hoof pads with hard, sharp edges. These allow it to run on hard rock or ice, as well as on soft snow.

European brown bears live in the mountains. They often make their homes in caves. Long, shaggy coats protect them from the cold. In the coldest part of winter, the bears hibernate, living off the energy stored in their body fat. To keep from using too much energy, their body temperature cools, and their heartbeats slow down.

People of the Mountains

Why do people live on cold, windy mountains? Thousands of years ago, mountain caves made natural homes. The cave homes were easy to defend against enemies and wild animals. Some people still make their homes in caves. But today, cave dwellings might have modern facilities. The mountains provide materials, such as wood and rock, to build houses, too.

Many mountain homes have small windows that keep out the cold. The roofs slope over the sides of the house. This catches the snow and keeps it from piling against the walls.

Transportation and communications are difficult in the mountains. Road and railroad tunnels and bridges have been made through mountains to avoid the slopes. Cable cars carry people to higher parts of the mountain.

Food on the mountains

Many animals can be found above the **tree line**. Sheep and goats provide mountain people with meat, milk, wool, and leather. Further down, farmers raise larger herds of sheep and cattle on sloping grasslands. Crops of hay are also grown there to feed the animals in the winter.

It is difficult to grow food crops on mountain slopes. Soil is often poor and gets washed away by the rain or blown away by the wind. Sometimes, it is just pulled slowly down the slope by gravity. This is known as soil creep. Farmers build flat steps, called terraces, with long walls to keep in soil and water. Terraces are found in mountain communities all over the world, from Peru to China. Many types of crops can be grown on terraces, from rice to grapes. Farmers grow an even greater variety of crops on the rich soils that cover the slopes of volcanoes.

◈ New Zealand sheep graze high in the mountains during the summer. In the autumn, shepherds round them up and take them down to the **foothills**. Some sheep are sold, but the rest are kept in the lowlands during the winter. There is more food for them there.

A Way of Life—Tibet

Tibet is a land in central Asia. It is hidden by mountains on three sides. Most Tibetans live on a very high **plateau** between the Karakoram Mountains in the west and the Kunlun range in the north. The Himalayas are to the south. The average height of the land is about 16,000 feet (4,875 meters) above sea level.

The Tibetan people have **adapted** to the cold temperatures and thin air. They do not suffer from **altitude** sickness, which is caused by a lack of oxygen in the blood. Tibetans also use the resources in their natural environment to make a living and build their homes.

Many of Asia's most important rivers begin in the Tibetan mountains. The rivers include the Ganges, Indus, Chang, Brahmaputra, Mekong, Sutlej, and Huang-He.

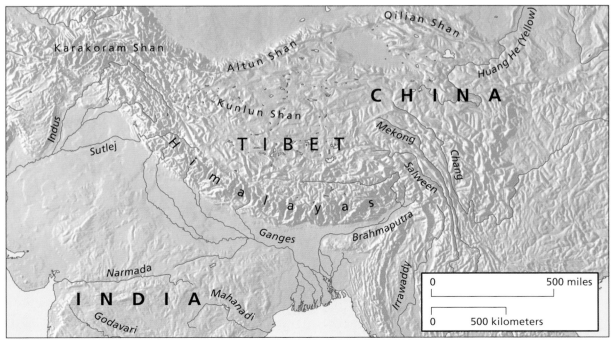

Building a home, making a living

Tibetan homes are made from mountain rock. They have thick walls and small windows to keep out the cold. Some Tibetans are nomads for at least part of the year. They travel with their herds of yaks, sheep, and goats to find the best pastures. They also raise cattle, horses, and shaggy-coated Bactrian camels.

Tibetans grow barley, wheat, rye, fruit, vegetables, and root crops, such as potatoes, on their farms. They often do their cooking outside on a stove made of stone with a wood fire below. Tsampa is a favorite dish, made of roasted barley seeds. Tibetans make wheat flour into dumplings, which are then stuffed with meat. Flour can also be made into noodles.

Some Tibetans make a living as mountain guides for tourists and climbers. They also carry the climbers' equipment. The mountains are full of **minerals** and gemstones, which Tibetans use in jewelry, but mining is not yet a big industry.

◈ The yak is a very important animal for Tibetans. Yak meat is roasted or dried to preserve it. The rich milk is made into butter, yogurt, cheese, and yak-butter tea, which can be drunk or mixed with barley tsampa. Yaks can be many colors. This is because they are often mixed, or cross-bred, with cattle.

Changing Mountains

Natural changes

Mountains are changing naturally all the time. The earth's **plates** are always moving apart or pushing together, making the mountains rise. Mountain blocks push up or slip down along the **faults** that lie in the earth's crust. Hot **magma** continues to force its way to the surface, adding to existing volcanoes or making new ones.

Mountains are always being **eroded,** too. This makes them continually change shape. The eroded material, such as fine soil and stones, gets swept down to the **valley** floor. Some **sediment** then gets carried away by rivers to the sea. Other sediment builds up into layers of sandstone and clay rocks when it is in the water. These rocks might one day be pushed or folded upward into new mountains, as the process begins again.

Bangladesh is a low-lying country in Asia. The Brahmaputra and Ganges Rivers flow slowly through Bangladesh and into the sea. Once a year, very heavy rain falls on the mountains far away where the rivers begin their courses. This makes the rivers flood. The waters are usually welcomed, because farmers can plant rice and other crops in the flooded fields. But in recent years the waters have risen too high. This has been partly caused by cutting down too many trees in the mountains. The people of Bangladesh can do nothing about this problem, as the mountains lie in other countries.

Human changes

The mountain environment has changed a lot, especially in recent times. Mining has cut great holes into the mountains. Trees have been cut down from the forests, leaving many mountainsides bare. **Habitats** of birds and mammals have been destroyed. The soil is no longer held together by tree roots, so it slips and washes down the slopes. Rain cannot sink into the soil, so it streams down the mountains and floods the valleys.

There are also many more **avalanches**. Trees help to keep the snow from slipping, so cutting down trees has partly caused the problem. So has **acid rain**, which has killed trees in many mountain forests. Some people think avalanches are caused by global warming. Global warming is a change in **climate** that is slowly warming the earth and melting the snow. Others think avalanches are caused by too many tourists skiing down the snowy slopes.

There is a lot of eroded material on this mountain. The stones and soil are called **scree**. This has happened naturally. It has changed the shape of the slope.

Looking to the Future

The process of mountains being uplifted and **eroded** will never end. The forces that make and shape mountains are largely beyond human control. But people can look after the environment in the mountains and **valleys**. This will make safe, healthy homes for plants, animals, and people.

A question of gas

Global warming might be having an effect on the world's mountains. But what are the causes of global warming, and how can it be stopped? Some scientists think that flares darting from the sun are making the earth hotter. We can do nothing about that. Others blame factories and cars that burn

What is the future for people living in the Alps at Chamonix, France? Chamonix is a very popular skiing resort. Buildings have been planned with safety in mind. There are concrete avalanche barriers 20 feet (6 meters) high. However, in February 1999, 79 inches (2 meters) of snow fell in just a few days. This led to devastating avalanches. The worst avalanche hit buildings in what was thought to be a "safe" area. There are many different factors that can cause avalanches. No one really knows who is to blame.

fossil fuels and release gases, such as carbon dioxide, into the air. These gases trap the sun's heat, warming the earth. They are called greenhouse gases. Releasing fewer harmful gases will reduce this effect. It will also help solve the problem of **acid rain** that is destroying many mountain forests.

Wearing away the mountains

Another problem is that people cut down too many trees. This has led to landslides, flooded valleys, and **avalanches**. One solutions is to cut down only older, mature trees and to replant with new trees. This is happening in many parts of the world.

Tourists are another problem for mountain environments. Hikers and climbers wear away plants and soil on mountain slopes. In parts of the United States, raised wooden walkways are used to protect the soil. But as more roads are built in the mountains to reach new tourist resorts, more soil erosion and landslides occur.

◇ Empty oxygen bottles and plastic packaging litter climbers' base camps on Mt. Everest. This kind of litter cannot dissolve or wash away. Trash is a growing problem on popular climbing peaks throughout the world.

27

Mountain Facts

On top of the world

The Himalayas in central Asia are home to the 20 highest peaks in the world. The next highest mountains are found in the **belts** stretching through North and South America. The list below shows the highest peaks on each continent.

Continent	Mountain (Range)	Height above sea level (feet)	(meters)
Asia	Everest (Himalayas)	29,035	8,850
South America	Aconcagua (Andes)	22,834	6,960
North America	McKinley (Rockies)	20,320	6,194
Africa	Kilimanjaro (Northern Highlands, Tanzania)	19,340	5,895
Oceania	Puncak Jaya (Pegunungan Maoke, New Guinea)	16,500	5,029
Antarctica	Vinson Massif (Ellsworth)	16,864	4,897
Europe	Mont Blanc (Alps)	15,771	4,807

Did you know that satellite pictures are used to measure the peaks of the tallest mountains? In 1999, a team of scientists used satellite equipment to discover that Mt. Everest is actually 29,035 feet (8850 meters) high, seven feet (two meters) higher than previously thought.

Beneath the waves

The longest underwater mountain range is the India and East Pacific Oceans **Cordillera**. It is over 12,000 miles (19,000 kilometers) long.

The peak of Mauna Kea, a volcanic mountain in Hawaii, rises only 13,792 feet (4,205 meters) above the water. The other 19,673 feet (5,998 meters) are under the ocean. When the two heights are combined, it makes Mauna Kea the tallest peak in the world.

Not so steep

The smallest hill in the world marked on official maps is in Brunei, in Asia. It is only 15 feet (4.5 meters) high and is part of a golf course.

Glossary

acid rain rain that has been polluted by gases from cars and factories

adapt to change to make suitable for a new use

algae simple form of plant life, ranging from a single cell to a huge seaweed

altitude height above sea level

avalanche mass of snow that slips down a mountainside

belt large group of mountain ranges (also called a cordillera)

camouflage color or pattern that makes an object blend in with its surroundings

climate rainfall, temperature, and wind that normally affect a large area

conifer tree that has cones to protect its seeds and normally keeps its spiny leaves throughout the year

continental drift movement of the earth's tectonic plates

cordillera large group of mountain ranges (also called a belt)

corrasion when stones get carried along by flowing water and bump against the river's bed and sides, causing erosion

crater hollow in the top of a volcano

current strong surge of water that flows constantly in one direction

erosion wearing away of rocks and soil by wind, water, ice, or acid

fault crack deep in the earth's crust

fertile describes rich soil in which plants grow easily

foothill any of the low hills around a mountain or mountain range

fossil fuels substances, including oil and gas, formed from the remains of plants and animals that lived millions of years ago

fungus type of simple plant, such as a mold or mushroom

glacier thick mass of ice, formed from compressed snow, that flows downhill

gorge narrow river valley with very steep sides

habitat place where a plant or animal lives or grows in nature

hibernate to sleep through the winter, using energy stored in body fat

igneous type of rock made of hardened magma

lava thick magma that has reached the air above ground and cooled

lichen not a true plant, but a mixture of a fungus and algae

magma layer of hot, melted rock beneath the hard crust of the earth

mantle layer of hot, melted rock on which the earth's crust sits

metamorphic type of rock that has been heated and compressed inside the earth's crust

mineral substance that is formed naturally in rocks and earth, such as coal, tin, or salt

molten melted by high temperatures

plate area of the earth's crust separated from other plates by deep cracks. Earthquakes, volcanic activity, and the forming of mountains take place where these plates meet.

plateau area of high, flat ground, often lying between mountains

plug solid, tube-shaped piece of volcanic rock that fills a volcano when the volcano dies or is dormant

range group of mountains formed at the same time and in a similar way

ridge long, narrow peak or range

scour to rub hard against something, wearing it away

scree small, loose stones covering a mountain slope

sediment fine soil and gravel that is carried in water

sedimentary type of rock made of layers of compressed clay and gritty sand that were once covered in water

species one of the groups used for classifying animals. The members of each species are very similar.

tree line highest part of a mountain on which trees can grow

valley scooped-out, low-lying area of land between mountains

watershed area of high ground surrounding a river's drainage basin

water vapor water that has been heated so much that it forms a gas that is held in the air. Drops of water form again when the vapor is cooled.

weathering action of weather on rock or other materials

More Books to Read

Green, Jen. *People of the Mountains.* Austin, Tex.: Raintree Steck-Vaughn, 1998.

Lovell, Scarlett, and Sue Smith. *Exploring Mountain Habitats.* Greenvale, N.Y.: Mondo Publishing, 1999.

Tesar, Jenny E. *America's Top 10 Mountains.* Woodbridge, Conn.: Blackbirch Press, Inc., 1997.

Vrbova, Zuza. *Mountains.* Mahwah, N.J.: Troll Communications, 1997.

Index

Aborigines   4
acid rain   25, 27
Aconcagua   28
Alaska   7, 15
algae   17
Alps   12, 17, 28
Andes Mountains   7, 28
Appalachian Mountains   12
Arctic foxes   19
Arctic hares   19
Atlantic Ocean   14
avalanches   25, 26, 27
Ayer's Rock   4

Bactrian camels   23
Balkan Mountains   17
Bangladesh   24
bears   19
Black Hills   9
block mountains 9
Brahmaputra River   22, 24
Brunei   29

Chamonix, France   26
climate   5, 7, 13, 15, 16, 25, 26,
   27
Colorado River   14
conifer trees   16, 17
continental drift   8
cordilleras   6, 7, 29

deserts   7
dome mountains   9

Earth's crust   4, 8, 9, 10, 24
"Enchanted City"   13
erosion   9, 11, 12, 13, 14, 24,
   26
Everest, Mt.   22, 27, 28

fold mountains   9
fungi   17

Ganges River   22, 24
glaciers   9, 12, 13, 14
goats   21, 23
golden eagles   15, 18
gorges   13, 14
Grand Canyon   12, 14
Great Australian Desert   6
Great Dividing Range,
   Australia   6
Great Salt Lake   15

Himalayas   6, 9, 21, 22, 28

igneous rocks   12

Karakoram Mountains   22
Kilimanjaro, Mt.   28
Kunlun Mountains   22

lakes   11, 14
lichens   17, 19
llamas   19

McKinley, Mt.   28
mammals   18, 19, 25
marmots   18
Mauna Kea, Hawaii   11, 29
Mauna Loa, Hawaii   10
metamorphic rocks   12
minerals   15, 23
Mississippi River   14
Missouri River   14
Mont Blanc   28

New Zealand   21

oceans   4, 7, 10, 29
Ozark Mountains   9

Pacific Ocean   6, 10, 14, 29
Paricutin, Mt.   10
plateaus   5, 6, 9
plates   4, 8, 24
Puncak Jaya   28
Pyrenees Mountains   17

Rocky Mountain National
   Park   15
Rocky Mountains   6, 9, 14, 15,
   19, 28

Sahara Desert   7
St Helens, Mt.   11
satellite pictures   28
scree   13, 25
sedimentary rocks   12
sheep   21, 23
Sierra Nevada   9
silver fir   17

terraces   21
Tibet   22, 23
tourism   4, 15, 26, 27
transport   20
tsampa   23
turpentine   17

Uluru   see Ayer's Rock
Ural Mountains, Russia   5

vegetation   15, 16, 17, 24
Vinson Massif   28
volcanoes   5, 6, 8, 10, 11

water vapor   13
weathering   12
worn mountains   9

yaks   19, 23

READ WELL®

All About Mammals

Teacher's Guide

Read Well 1 · Unit 11

H̲ says /h/.
Quick Sound (not huh)
Unvoiced/Quiet

Critical Foundations in Primary Reading

Marilyn Sprick, Lisa Howard, Ann Fidanque, Shelley V. Jones

ISBN 1-59318-409-3

10 09 08   11 10 9 8 7

SOPRIS WEST™ EDUCATIONAL SERVICES
A CAMBIUM LEARNING COMPANY

BOSTON, MA • LONGMONT, CO

Table of Contents
Unit 11
All About Mammals

Read Well 1 Sequence and Sound Pronunciation Guide iv

Introduction 1
New and Important Objectives. 2
Daily Lesson Planning. 4
Materials and Materials Preparation 6

Important Tips
Smooth and Bumpy Blending With <u>Hh</u> 8
Building Oral Reading Fluency. 9
Language Priming—Using Possessives. 10

How to Teach the Lessons
Decoding Practice 1 12
Storybook Introduction 14
Story 1, Duet 16
Skill Work Activity 1 21
Story 2, Solo 22
Comprehension Work Activity 2. 25

Decoding Practice 2. 26
Story 3, Duet 28
Skill Work Activity 3 33
Story 4, Solo 34
Comprehension Work Activity 4. 37

How to Teach the Lessons (*continued*)

Decoding Practice 3 38
Story 5, Duet 40
Skill Work Activity 5 45
Story 6, Solo 46
Fact Summary 49
Skill Work Activity 6 51

Decoding Practice 4 52

End of the Unit

Making Decisions 55
Unit 11 Decoding Assessment 56
Certificate of Achievement and Goal Setting 57

Extra Practice 1 58
Extra Practice 1 Blackline Master 59
Extra Practice Activity 1 Blackline Masters 60

Extra Practice 2 62
Extra Practice 2 Blackline Master 63
Extra Practice Activity 2 Blackline Master 64

Extra Practice 3, 4 65
Extra Practice Activity 3 Blackline Masters 66
Extra Practice Activity 4 Blackline Master 68

I I Voiced (Word) **Unit A**	**Mm** /mmm/ Monkey Continuous Voiced **Unit B**	**Ss** /sss/ Snake Continuous Unvoiced **Unit 1**	**Ee** /eee/ Emu Continuous Voiced (Long) **Unit 2**	**ee** /eeee/ Bee Continuous Voiced (Long) **Unit 2**	**Mm** /mmm/ Monkey Continuous Voiced **Unit 3**
Aa /aaa/ Ant Continuous Voiced (Short) **Unit 4**	**Dd** /d/ Dinosaur Quick Voiced (not duh) **Unit 5**	**th** /ththth/ the Continuous Voiced **Unit 6**	**Nn** /nnn/ Nest Continuous Voiced **Unit 7**	**Tt** /t/ Turkey Quick Unvoiced (not tuh) **Unit 8**	**Ww** /www/ Wind Continuous Voiced (woo) **Unit 9**
Ii /iii/ Insects Continuous Voiced (Short) **Unit 10**	**Th** /Ththth/ The Continuous Voiced **Unit 10**	**Hh** /h/ Hippo Quick Unvoiced (not huh) **Unit 11**	**Cc** /c/ Cat Quick Unvoiced (not cuh) **Unit 12**	**Rr** /rrr/ Rabbit Continuous Voiced **Unit 13**	**ea** /eaeaea/ Eagle Continuous Voiced (Long) **Unit 13**
Sh/sh /shshsh/ Sheep Continuous Unvoiced **Unit 14**	**Kk, -ck** /k/ Kangaroo Quick Unvoiced (not kuh) **Unit 15**	**oo** /oooo/ Moon Continuous Voiced (Long) **Unit 16**	**ar** /ar/ Shark Voiced (R-Controlled) **Unit 17**	**Wh/wh** /wh/ Whale Quick Voiced **Unit 18**	**Ee** /ĕĕĕ/ Engine or Ed Continuous Voiced (Short) **Unit 19**
-y /-yyy/ Fly Continuous Voiced (Long) **Unit 20**	**Ll** /lll/ Letter Continuous Voiced **Unit 21**	**Oo** /ooo/ Otter Continuous Voiced (Short) **Unit 22**	**Bb** /b/ Bat Quick Voiced (not buh) **Unit 23**	**all** /all/ Ball Voiced **Unit 23**	**Gg** /g/ Gorilla Quick Voiced (not guh) **Unit 24**
Ff /fff/ Frog Continuous Unvoiced **Unit 25**	**Uu** /uuu/ Umbrella Continuous Voiced (Short) **Unit 26**	**er** /er/ Sister Voiced (R-Controlled) **Unit 27**	**oo** /oo/ Book Voiced (Short) **Unit 27**	**Yy** /y-/ Yarn Quick Voiced **Unit 28**	**Aa** /a/ Ago Voiced (Schwa) **Unit 28**
Pp /p/ Pig Quick Unvoiced (not puh) **Unit 29**	**ay** /ay/ Hay Voiced **Unit 29**	**Vv** /vvv/ Volcano Continuous Voiced **Unit 30**	**Qu/qu** /qu/ Quake Quick Unvoiced **Unit 31**	**Jj** /j/ Jaguar Quick Voiced (not juh) **Unit 32**	**Xx** /ksss/ Fox Continuous Unvoiced **Unit 33**
or /or/ Horn Voiced (R-Controlled) **Unit 33**	**Zz** /zzz/ Zebra Continuous Voiced **Unit 34**	**a_e** /a_e/ Cake Bossy E Voiced (Long) **Unit 34**	**-y** /-y/ Baby Voiced **Unit 35**	**i_e** /i_e/ Kite Bossy E Voiced (Long) **Unit 35**	**ou** /ou/ Cloud Voiced **Unit 36**
ow /ow/ Cow Voiced **Unit 36**	**Ch/ch** /ch/ Chicken Quick Unvoiced **Unit 37**	**ai** /ai/ Rain Voiced (Long) **Unit 37**	**igh** /igh/ Flight Voiced (Long) **Unit 38**	**o_e** /o_e/ Bone Bossy E Voiced (Long) **Unit 38**	**ir** /ir/ Bird Voiced (R-Controlled) **Unit 38**

Introduction
All About Mammals

Story Notes

In this unit, young readers read their first nonfiction passage. While acquiring background knowledge and vocabulary from the sciences, students will enjoy *reading to learn*. What makes a mammal a mammal? Is an elephant a mammal? Is a whale a mammal? What is a habitat?

Recommended Read Aloud

For reading outside of small group instruction

Animals Born Alive and Well by Ruth Heller

Nonfiction • Narrative Poem

Animals Born Alive and Well is a nature book in verse. Children learn that "Mammals are animals with fur or hair, who nurse their young, and breathe fresh air." On each page Heller depicts animals—from wild to tame, from common to exotic.

Read Well Connection

In *All About Mammals* children learn additional information about the classification of mammals. The *Read Well* stories in this unit complement Heller's *Animals Born Alive and Well*. Each passage reinforces and enriches the knowledge learned from the other. Watch for connections between the two books.

NOTE FROM THE AUTHORS

Cheer your children along. Your enthusiasm is contagious. Provide specific and descriptive feedback: You know what a mammal is. You can name different mammals, and you can even figure out whether an animal is a mammal. I am very proud of you.

New and Important Objectives

A Research-Based Reading Program
Just Right for Young Children

Oral Language
Phonemic Awareness
Phonics
Fluency
Vocabulary
Comprehension

◆◆ Oral Language

Language patterns can be found in Stretch and Shrink, Smooth and Bumpy Blending, Sounding Out Smoothly, and Dictation. Continue practice throughout the day. Prompt students who would benefit from additional oral language practice to use the language patterns during instruction. (See page 10 for a list of the Unit 11 Oral Language Patterns.)

Phonemic Awareness

Isolating Beginning, Middle, Ending Sounds,
Segmenting, Blending, Manipulating, Rhyming, Onset and Rime

Phonics

Letter Sounds and Combinations
★ Hh
Review • Ss, Ee, ee, Mm, Aa, Dd, th, Nn, Tt, Ww, Ii, Th

· ·

Pattern Words
Note: Words from Unit 11 forward are listed alphabetically.
★ Dad's, ★ Dee, ★ dim, ★ had, ★ Had, ★ hand, ★ hat, ★ he, ★ He, ★ Heed, ★ hid, ★ Hid, ★ him, ★ Him, ★ mint, ★ mitt, ★ needs, ★ Sam's, ★ swim, ★ swims, ★ That
Review • an, and, at, dad, Dan, I'm, in, mad, man, mat, me, meet, Meet, Nan, need, needs, sad, Sam, sand, sat, see, See, seem, seems, sees, sit, Than, that, This, Tim, we, We, Weed

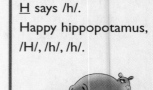

H says /h/.
Happy hippopotamus,
/H/, /h/, /h/.

· ·

Tricky Words
★ as, ★ has, ★ his, ★ His, ★ is, ★ with
Review • I, said, the, The, was

Quick Sound (not huh)

◆◆ = Oral language patterns   ★ = New in this unit

Comprehension

Comprehension Strategies

Building Knowledge, Priming Background Knowledge, Making Connections, Predicting, Identifying, Describing, Defining, Applying, Explaining, Inferring, Classifying, Questioning, Summarizing

. . . .

Story Elements

Title, Who (Character), What (Action)

. . . .

Story Vocabulary

★Whale, ★Camel, ★Hippo, ★Mammals, ★Habitat

. . . .

Expository Elements

★Topic, ★Fact

. . . .

Genre

★Nonfiction • Expository (Student-read)

Fiction • Narrative With Factual Content

. . . .

Lessons

★Facts provide fun food for thought.

★Facts can help you identify and classify mammals.

. . . .

Written Response

Sentence Copying, Sentence Illustration, Sentence Completion, Sentence Comprehension—Multiple Choice

Fluency

Accuracy, Expression, Rate

Daily Lesson Planning

PACING

Some students will begin the process of learning to read slowly but make rapid progress later. To be at grade level by the end of the year, first graders need to complete Unit 20 by the end of the 18th week of school. Groups that are working at a slower pace may require more intensive *Read Well* instruction and practice. (See *Getting Started: A Guide to Implementation.*)

ASSESSMENT

Upon completion of this unit, assess each student and proceed to Unit 12 as appropriate.

SAMPLE LESSON PLANS

The sample lesson plans illustrate how materials can be used for students with different learning needs. Each lesson plan is designed to provide daily decoding practice and story reading.

> **A BASIC RULE (Reminder)**
> Make adjustments frequently, moving students as quickly as possible without sacrificing mastery.

2-DAY PLAN • *Acceleration*

Day 1	Day 2
• Decoding Practice 1 • Stories 1 and 2 • Skill Work 1* • Comprehension Work 2* • Homework 1, Story 2*	• Decoding Practice 2 • Stories 3 and 4 and Fact Summary • Skill Work 3* • Comprehension Work 4* • Homework 2, Story 4* • Homework 3, Story 6*

In this 2-Day Plan, students skip Decoding Practice 3, Decoding Practice 4, and Stories 5 and 6. (Story 6 is included in the homework schedule.)

Hearing Sounds and Rhyming Patterns, Skill Work 5 and 6, can be used any time during the unit as independent work.

3-DAY PLAN

Day 1	Day 2	Day 3
• Decoding Practice 1 • Stories 1 and 2 • Skill Work 1* • Comprehension Work 2* • Homework 1, Story 2*	• Decoding Practice 2 • Stories 3 and 4 • Skill Work 3* • Comprehension Work 4* • Homework 2, Story 4*	• Decoding Practice 3 • Stories 5 and 6 and Fact Summary • Skill Work 5* • Skill Work 6* • Homework 3, Story 6* • Homework 4, Storybook Decoding Review*

4-DAY PLAN

Day 1	Day 2	Day 3	Day 4
• Decoding Practice 1 • Stories 1 and 2 • Skill Work 1* • Comprehension Work 2* • Homework 1, Story 2*	• Decoding Practice 2 • Stories 3 and 4 • Skill Work 3* • Comprehension Work 4* • Homework 2, Story 4*	• Decoding Practice 3 • Stories 5 and 6 and Fact Summary • Skill Work 5* • Homework 3, Story 6*	• Decoding Practice 4 • Review Stories 2, 4, and 6 • Skill Work 6* • Homework 4, Storybook Decoding Review*

* From *Read Well* Comprehension and Skill Work (workbook), *Read Well* Homework (blackline masters), or Extra Practice in this book.

4

6-DAY PLAN • *Pre-Intervention*

Day 1	**Day 2**	**Day 3**
• Decoding Practice 1 • Story 1 • Skill Work 1*	• Review Decoding Practice 1 • Story 2 • Comprehension Work 2* • Homework 1, Story 2*	• Decoding Practice 2 • Story 3 • Skill Work 3*
Day 4	**Day 5**	**Day 6**
• Review Decoding Practice 2 • Story 4 • Comprehension Work 4* • Homework 2, Story 4*	• Decoding Practice 3 • Story 5 • Skill Work 5* • Homework 4, Storybook Decoding Review*	• Decoding Practice 4 • Story 6 and Fact Summary • Skill Work 6* • Homework 3, Story 6*

PRE-INTERVENTION AND INTERVENTION

See *Getting Started: A Guide to Implementation* for information on how to achieve mastery at a faster pace with students who require six or more days of instruction.

8-DAY PLAN • *Intervention*

Day 1	**Day 2**	**Day 3**	**Day 4**
• Decoding Practice 1 • Story 1 • Skill Work 1*	• Review Decoding Practice 1 • Story 2 • Comprehension Work 2* • Homework 1, Story 2*	• Decoding Practice 2 • Story 3 • Skill Work 3*	• Review Decoding Practice 2 • Story 4 • Comprehension Work 4* • Homework 2, Story 4*
Day 5	**Day 6**	**Day 7**	**Day 8**
• Decoding Practice 3 • Story 5 • Skill Work 5* • Homework 4, Storybook Decoding Review*	• Decoding Practice 4 • Story 6 and Fact Summary • Skill Work 6* • Homework 3, Story 6*	• Extra Practice 1* • Extra Practice Activity 1*	• Extra Practice 2* • Extra Practice Activity 2*

10-DAY PLAN • *Intervention*

Day 1	**Day 2**	**Day 3**	**Day 4**	**Day 5**
• Decoding Practice 1 • Story 1 • Skill Work 1*	• Review Decoding Practice 1 • Story 2 • Comprehension Work 2* • Homework 1, Story 2*	• Decoding Practice 2 • Story 3 • Skill Work 3*	• Review Decoding Practice 2 • Story 4 • Comprehension Work 4* • Homework 2, Story 4*	• Decoding Practice 3 • Story 5 • Skill Work 5* • Homework 4, Storybook Decoding Review*
Day 6	**Day 7**	**Day 8**	**Day 9**	**Day 10**
• Decoding Practice 4 • Story 6 and Fact Summary • Skill Work 6* • Homework 3, Story 6*	• Extra Practice 1* • Extra Practice Activity 1*	• Extra Practice 2* • Extra Practice Activity 2*	• Extra Practice 3 • Storybook Decoding Review • Review Solos: Units 8 and 9** • Extra Practice Activity 3*	• Extra Practice 4 • Review Decoding Practice 4 • Review Solos: Units 10 and 11** • Extra Practice Activity 4*

** Use review stories as listed or substitute with stories from *Read Well K*, Unit 11.

Materials and Materials Preparation

 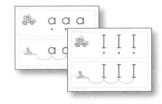  

Core Lessons

Teacher Materials

READ WELL MATERIALS

- Unit 11 Teacher's Guide
- Sound and Word Cards for Units 1–11
- Smooth and Bumpy Blending Cards 19, 21, 22, 23
- Spring toys (optional for use with Stretch and Shrink)
- Game markers (optional for use with cover-up activities)
- *Assessment Manual* or page 56

SCHOOL SUPPLIES

- Stopwatch or watch with a second hand

Student Materials

READ WELL MATERIALS

- Decoding Book 2 for each student
- Unit 11 Storybook for each student
- Unit 11 Comprehension and Skill Work for each student (My Activity Book 2)
- Unit 11 Certificate of Achievement (blackline master page 57)
- Unit 11 Homework for each student (blackline masters)
  See *Getting Started* for suggested homework routines.

SCHOOL SUPPLIES

- Pencils, colors (optional—markers, crayons, or colored pencils)

Make one copy per student of each blackline master as appropriate for the group.

Note: For new or difficult Comprehension and Skill Work activities, make overhead transparencies from the blackline masters. Use the transparencies to demonstrate and guide practice.

Extra Practice Lessons

Note: Use these lessons only if needed.

Student Materials

READ WELL MATERIALS

- Unit 11 Extra Practice 1 and 2 for each student (blackline master pages 59 and 63)
- Unit 11 Extra Practice Activities 1, 2, 3, and 4 for each student (blackline master pages 60–61 double-sided; 64; 66–67 single-sided; 68)

SCHOOL SUPPLIES

- Pencils, colors (markers, crayons, or colored pencils), highlighters, scissors, glue
- White boards or paper

Important Tips

In this section, you will find:

★ **Smooth and Bumpy Blending With <u>Hh</u>**

/H/ is both quick and unvoiced, making blending difficult. A fully scripted lesson is provided on page 8 so you can study, rehearse, and visualize how to teach this skill—prior to working with children.

★ **Building Oral Reading Fluency**

Read Well students gradually become fluent readers as they learn to process print. Learn how to guide the development of accurate, automatic, and expressive reading.

★ **Language Priming—Using Possessives**

Use the information on page 10 to encourage English Language Learners (ELL students) and children with language delays to use possessives in their oral language.

★Smooth and Bumpy Blending With <u>Hh</u>

PRONUNCIATION

The letter <u>Hh</u> is both a quick (or stop) sound and unvoiced. Teach students to say an unvoiced /h/, not /huh/. The /huh/ pronunciation makes word recognition unnecessarily difficult, e.g., /huhaaammm/ vs. /haaammm/.

BLENDING

Bumpy Blending prepares students for the more difficult Smooth Blending. With Smooth Blending, children are taught to pronounce /h/ and the adjoining vowel as one sound. With the word "he" you will demonstrate and guide blending by looping directly to /eee/. The whole word is blended in one continuous breath as follows: /heee/.

Use Blending Card 22 to teach students how to blend letter <u>h</u>.

BLENDING CARD 22

- Demonstrate Bumpy Blending of *he*.
  I'm going to do Bumpy Blending.
  Tap under each letter. /h/ • /e/
  The word is "he."
  Look at [Julian]. What is *he* doing? (*He* is [reading].)
- Guide Bumpy Blending of *he*.
  Everyone, let's do Bumpy Blending together.
  Tap under each letter. /h/ • /e/
- Repeat with group and individual turns, independent of your voice.
- Demonstrate Smooth Blending of *he*.
  I'm going to do Smooth Blending.
  Loop to the letter <u>e</u>. /heee/
- Guide Smooth Blending of *he*.
  Let's do Smooth Blending together.
  Loop to the letter <u>e</u>. /heee/
  Say the word. (he)
- Repeat with group and individual turns, independent of your voice.

★Building Oral Reading Fluency

FLUENCY

Fluent reading is characteristic of a reader who is free of word-identification problems that often hinder comprehension. As students master the blending process, many students develop fluency with ease, while other students require additional practice.

ADDITIONAL PRACTICE

When students need additional practice to meet the desired fluency on assessments, work first on accuracy and then on rate. Five extra minutes with a trained instructional assistant, parent volunteer, or older student can ensure success for many high-risk students. Early intervention can pre-empt later remediation.

INDIVIDUAL INTERVENTIONS: ACCURACY

In addition to Blending Practice and Dictation, have students read Solo Stories, Homework, and Extra Practice.

- Use the Personal Goal Setting form on page 57 to establish an accuracy goal.
- Have students practice a story with repeated readings. Encourage children to sound out difficult words, rather than blurting out incorrect responses.

  As the student reads, draw a star above each word read or sounded out correctly. (Use a transparent overlay if using Solo Stories.)

  Between readings, have the student practice blending any missed words.

  Then, have the student reread the story. Draw a star above each word read correctly that was missed on the first reading.

INDIVIDUAL INTERVENTIONS: FLUENCY

Once students can read a passage accurately, work on fluency—accuracy *and* rate.

With Solo, Homework, and Extra Practice Activities:
Have the student read a story for 30 seconds. Mark errors. To determine words correct per minute (wcpm), count the words read *correctly*, then multiply times two.

Have the student practice two or three sentences at a time. Model and guide expressive and accurate reading.

Have the student try for his or her personal best with two or three additional timed readings on the same passage. (A chart is provided on Extra Practice Activity 2.)

★Language Priming Using Possessives

For English Language Learners and Children With Language Delays

Continued review and attention to the language patterns in *Read Well* can augment a more formal language intervention. With this lesson, children learn to use possessives in their oral language.

EXAMPLE: Students are introduced to the statement/question/ response pattern: This is [Sam]'s [dad]. Whose [dad] is it? ([Sam's])

Practice the statement/question/response pattern.
This is [Martha]'s [book]. Whose [book] is it? ([Martha's])
Say the whole sentence, starting with "This is."
(This is [Martha's] book.)

Watch for natural opportunities to engage English Language Learners with the oral language pattern.
I found a coat on the playground.
[Kyoshi], do you know whose coat this is? ([Jeremy's])
[Jeremy], is this your coat? (Yes)
[Kyoshi], you were right. This is [Jeremy's] coat.

Exercises that include repeating language patterns are marked with ◆◆s.

ORAL LANGUAGE PATTERNS	
Introduced in This Unit and Reviewed From Previous Units	
★ Yesterday, we *had* . . . [fun].	★ The [hippo] *swims* in the [river].
★ The dog *hid* under the bed.	★ That's *Dad's* [car]. Whose [car] is it? (*Dad's*)
★ What *can* we do? (We *can* [read].)	Look at [Julian]. What is *he* doing? (*He* is [reading].)
★ What does a *cat* say? (A *cat* says "meow.")	Look at [Dillon]. See *him* [read].
★ What do you do in a swimming pool? (*Swim*)	We are *in* the classroom.
★ That's *Sam's* [dad]. Whose [dad] is it? (*Sam's*)	[Thomas] *seems* [happy].
★ What did the *kid* do? ([She ran home.])	This apple tastes good. It is *sweet* and juicy.
★ What does a mad *cat* do? (*Hiss*)	We are [reading]. What are *we* doing?
★ See the cat and the . . . (*hat*).	What is *this*? (*This* is a [pencil].)
★ [Katie] *needs* [help]. What does [she] need?	This is a *tin* can.
★ The [hippo] *hasn't* had lunch. Has [he] had lunch? (No)	What do you *need*? (I *need* [help].)
★ The [dog] *didn't* [bark]. Did [he] bark? (No)	You *seem* hungry but it's not time for lunch.

★ = New in this unit

How to Teach the Lessons

★ Stars signal new skills, activities, or stories. ★

Teach from this section. Each instructional component is outlined in an easy-to-teach format. Special tips are provided to help you nurture student progress.

In this section, you will find:

Decoding Practice 1

- Storybook Introduction
- Story 1, Duet
- Skill Work Activity 1
- Story 2, Solo
- Comprehension Work Activity 2

Decoding Practice 2

- Story 3, Duet
- Skill Work Activity 3
- Story 4, Solo
- Comprehension Work Activity 4

Decoding Practice 3

- Story 5, Duet
- Skill Work Activity 5
- Story 6, Solo
- Fact Summary
- Skill Work Activity 6

Decoding Practice 4

Review Solo Stories

SCAFFOLDED INSTRUCTION
Developmental Shift

As children gain confidence across units, begin with guided practice or independent practice, as appropriate.

If a word is new or different, you may wish to begin with a demonstration and guided practice.

11

① SOUND REVIEW

② NEW SOUND INTRODUCTION
Note: /h/ is both unvoiced and quick.

③ NEW SOUND PRACTICE

◆◆ **④ STRETCH AND SHRINK**

had-haaad-had	Yesterday, we *had* . . . (fun).
hid-hiiid-hid	The dog *hid* under the bed.
can-caaannn-can	What *can* we do? (We *can* [read].)
cat-caaat-cat	What does a *cat* say? (A *cat* says "meow.")

◆◆ **⑤ SMOOTH AND BUMPY BLENDING—CARDS 22, 23**

◆◆ **⑥ SOUNDING OUT SMOOTHLY**
For each word in the Flower Column, have students blend /h/ with the vowel first, sound out the word, and then read the word: Heee-He; haaa-haaad-had; hiii-hiiimmm-him.
Use the words in sentences as needed.

✿	*Heee-He*	Look at [Julian]. What is *he* doing? (*He* is [reading].)
	haaad-had	Yesterday, we *had* . . . [fun].
	hiiimmm-him	Look at [Dillon]. See *him* [read].
♥	*Wwweee-We*	What are *we* doing? (*We* are [reading].)
	Thththiiisss-This	What is *this?* (*This* is a [pencil].)
●	*Daaannn-Dan*	*Dan* is a boy's name. Are you *Dan?* ([No])
	ssswwwiiimmm-swim	What do you do in a swimming pool? (Swim)

★ **⑦ POSSESSIVE 'S**
"Sam's" is the first word students read with the possessive 's. Say something like:
Remember, you can sound out words with the little mark called an apostrophe.
Let's sound out the words then read them. /Sssaaammmsss/, Sam's, /daaad/, dad
Let's read the phrase. Sam's dad
The apostrophe tells us something belongs to Sam. Whose dad is he? (Sam's)

⑧ TRICKY WORDS
★ **New words: "is," "his," "as," "has"**
• Tell students their first new Tricky Word starts with /i/ and says "is." Have students say "is" five times. Use "is" in a sentence. A hippo <u>is</u> a mammal.
• Tell students "his" rhymes with "is." Follow the procedures used with "is."
• Repeat with "as" and "has."
• Repeat practice on the row. Mix group and individual turns, independent of your voice.

⑨ DAILY STORY READING
Proceed to the Unit 11 Storybook. See Daily Lesson Planning for pacing suggestions.

⑩ COMPREHENSION AND SKILL WORK ACTIVITY 1 AND/OR ACTIVITY 2
See pages 21 and/or 25.

UNIT 11 DECODING PRACTICE 1
(For use with Stories 1 and 2)

1. SOUND REVIEW Use Sound Cards for Units 1–10.

2. NEW SOUND INTRODUCTION Have students echo (repeat) the phrases. Do not have students read the poem.

H as in Hippo
Capital letter H, small letter h,
H says h.
Happy hippopotamus,
H, h, h.

WORKING TOWARD MASTERY
Repeat practice with each exercise to build mastery. Mix group and individual turns, independent of your voice.

SOUNDING OUT WITH /H/
Sounding out with the beginning sound /h/ is very difficult. The exercise in the Flower Column will help students learn to blend with /h/. If students have difficulty, have them start by identifying the vowel in each word.

3. NEW SOUND PRACTICE Have students read the sound, then trace and say the sound.

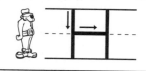 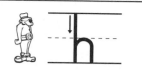

4. STRETCH AND SHRINK Have students orally Stretch and Shrink, then use each word in a sentence.

had-haaad-had
hid-hiiid-hid
can-caaannn-can
cat-caaat-cat

Do not have students read the words.

5. SMOOTH AND BUMPY BLENDING Use Blending Cards 22 and 23.

6. SOUNDING OUT SMOOTHLY For each word, have students say the underlined part, sound out the word in one smooth breath, then read the word.

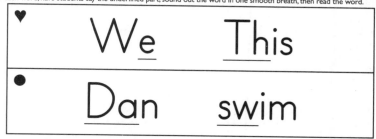

❀ He

had

him

♥ We   This

● Dan   swim

★7. POSSESSIVE 'S Have students sound out each word, then read the phrase.

☆ ★Sam's dad

★8. TRICKY WORDS Introduce "is," "his," "as," and "has" using basic Tricky Word procedure. Next, have students silently figure out each word, then read it aloud.

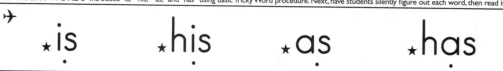

★is   ★his   ★as   ★has

9. DAILY STORY READING

5

① INTRODUCING THE STORYBOOK—COVER

Identifying—What

Ask students what they see on the cover of the book.

Identifying—Title

Tell students the title of the book is *Mammals*.

② INTRODUCING THE TITLE PAGE

Teacher Think Aloud—Priming Background Knowledge

The book is called *Mammals*.

Everyone, say that word "mammals." (Mammals)

Mammals are a special kind of animal.

In this book, the first story is called "What Makes an Animal a Mammal?" In this story, we're going to learn how to tell whether an animal is a mammal. The second story is called "More About Mammals." What do you think we're going to learn about in that story?

③ INTRODUCING "THIS IS A . . ." AND "THIS IS NOT A . . ."

Classifying

Note: In this exercise, students identify animals using positive and negative statements. "Is it a dog? This is not a dog. This is a whale." Through experience with simple examples, students practice the language and process of classification.

Follow the gray text on the bottom of the page.

> ◆◆ **LANGUAGE PRIMING**
>
> If you are working with English Language Learners, read the tip on page 10. A sample lesson is provided to help students understand and practice the use of positive and negative statements.

All About Mammals

By Marilyn Sprick and Ann Fidanque
Illustrated by Dan McGeehan

• This is a . . .
• This is not a . . .

whale   camel   hippo

Touch under the first picture. Is it a dog? (No)
Say "this is not a dog." (This is not a dog.)
Is it a cat? (No) Say "this is not a cat." (This is not a cat.)
Is this a whale? (Yes) Say "this is a whale." (This is a whale.)

Touch under the second picture. Is it a dog? (No)
Say "this is not a dog." (This is not a dog.)
Is this a camel? (Yes) Say "this is a camel." (This is a camel.)

Touch under the next picture. Is it a cat? (No)
Say "this is not a cat." (This is not a cat.)
Is this a hippo? (Yes) Say "this is a hippo." (This is a hippo.)

UNIT 11 STORIES

What Makes an Animal a Mammal?
Chapter 1, Mammal Facts 8
Chapter 2, The Whale 12

More About Mammals
Chapter 1, Mammals in Their Habitats 14
Chapter 2, The Camel Sat 18
Chapter 3, A Hippo Named Sam 20
Chapter 4, With His Dad 24
Fact Summary 26
Storybook Decoding Review 27

6

7

• **This is a . . .**
• **This is not a . . .**

  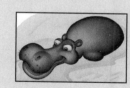

whale   camel   hippo

Touch under the first picture. Is it a dog? (No)
Say "this is not a dog." (This is not a dog.)
Is it a cat? (No) Say "this is not a cat." (This is not a cat.)
Is this a whale? (Yes) Say "this is a whale." (This is a whale.)

Touch under the second picture. Is it a dog? (No)
Say "this is not a dog." (This is not a dog.)
Is this a camel? (Yes) Say "this is a camel." (This is a camel.)

Touch under the next picture. Is it a cat? (No)
Say "this is not a cat." (This is not a cat.)
Is this a hippo? (Yes) Say "this is a hippo." (This is a hippo.)

DUET STORY READING INSTRUCTIONS

Students read from their own storybooks.

The teacher reads the small text and students read the large text.

PACING

- 2- to 4-Day Plans: Have students do the first reading of Duet Story 1.

  Then proceed to repeated readings of Solo Story 2.
- 6- to 10-Day Plans: Have students do the first *and* second readings.

COMPREHENSION BUILDING: DISCUSSION QUESTIONS AND TEACHER THINK ALOUDS

Ask questions and discuss text on the first or second reading when indicated in the storybook in light gray text.

PROCEDURES

1. First Reading

Have students identify the picture words {elephant}, {dog}, {whale}, and {lion}; then choral read the student text.

2. Second Reading

Have students take turns, with each student reading one line of student text.

What Makes an Animal a Mammal? [1]

CHAPTER 1
Mammal Facts

What do you think this story will be about? [2](Mammals)
Listen carefully for four facts about mammals.

Some animals are called mammals. Mammals have a backbone and breathe air. They have hair or fur, and they take care of their babies after they are born.

Tell four facts you just learned about mammals. [3](They have a backbone. They breathe air. They have hair or fur, and they take care of their babies after they are born.)

Cows, tigers, squirrels, and monkeys are all mammals.

8

IDENTIFYING FACTS

Students will use the facts about mammals presented in paragraph one to classify animals.

As you read the first paragraph, hold up a finger each time you identify a fact. After asking students to identify the facts, hold up a finger each time students name a fact.

Review as Needed

If students have difficulty naming the facts, reread the first paragraph. Have students recite each fact after it is presented. Then have them review all four facts.

❶ **Building Knowledge**
❷ **Predicting—Topic**
❸ **Identifying—Facts**

This is an .

The is an animal with a backbone.

He has a nose and breathes air.

He has a few hairs on his head.

Elephants live together and take care of their babies.
Does an elephant have a backbone? [1] (Yes)
Does an elephant breathe air? [2] (Yes)
Does an elephant have hair or fur? [3] (Yes)
Look at the picture. Do you think an elephant takes care of its babies? [4] (Yes)
So, an elephant is a . . [5] (mammal).

9

❶ **Summarizing**
❷ **Summarizing**
❸ **Summarizing**
❹ **Inferring**
❺ **Classifying**

FINGER TRACKING
(Reminder)
Continue having students track
the large text with their fingers.

STORY 1, DUET

What is a mammal? Touch the animals you think are mammals and say,

"**this is** a mammal," or "this is not a mammal."

Make a good guess. You may be surprised!

The 🐕, the 🐦, the 🦁, and the man are mammals.

So, what do you know about these animals?[1] (They have backbones. They breathe air. They have hair or fur. They take care of their young.)

10

❶ Inferring, Applying

Note: Questions focus students on important story elements and provide prompts for story discussions. Answers provide guidance, not verbatim responses.

I knew that a whale breathed air, but I didn't know it had hair or fur.**1** What would you like to learn about a whale?**2** (I'd like to learn where a whale has hair.)

Look at the bird. It has no fur or hair. Instead, a bird has feathers.
A bird is not a . . . mammal.**3** A bird is a bird.

Look at the fish. Fish do not breathe air, and they do not have fur or hair.
A fish is not a . . . mammal.**4** A fish is a fish.

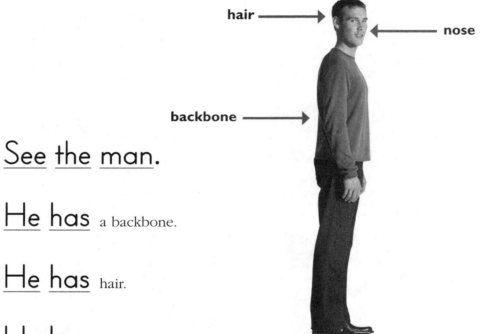

hair ———→

←——— nose

backbone ———→

See the man.

He has a backbone.

He has hair.

He has a nose and breathes air.

When the man was young, his parents took care of him.
Now the man helps take care of his children.
So, what do you know about the man?**5** (The man is a mammal.)
That's right. People are mammals.

Mammals can be found all over the world. Mammals live in forests, deserts, and a few mammals even live in the sea.

SUMMARIZING AND MAKING CONNECTIONS

After reading the page, say something like:

You learned some interesting facts about mammals. What are we? (Mammals)

Do you have a backbone? (Yes)
Touch your backbone.

Do you breathe air? (Yes)
Show me what you do when you breathe air.

Do you have hair? (Yes)
Touch your hair.

Who takes care of you?

We are . . . (mammals).

11

❶ **Teacher Think Aloud**

❷ **Questioning**

❸ **Classifying**

❹ **Classifying**

❺ **Applying, Classifying**

SOUND PAGE

Use work pages from the workbook.

UNIT II SKILL WORK ACTIVITY I
SOUND PAGE: For use after Story I

Name _____

© Sopris West Educational Services. All rights reserved.

7

CHECKOUT OPPORTUNITY

While students are working on Comprehension and Skill Work, you may wish to listen to individuals read a Decoding Practice or Solo Story. If the student makes an error, gently correct and have the student reread the column, row, or sentence.

PROCEDURES

For each step, demonstrate and guide practice as needed.

1. Handwriting—Basic Instructions

- Have students identify the capital letter <u>H</u> as in "Hippo."
- Have students trace and write the capital letter <u>H</u>—leaving a finger space between each letter. Repeat with small letter <u>h</u> on the next two rows.

2. Drawing Pictures That Begin With /h/—Basic Instructions

- Have students brainstorm possible items.
  Examples: hand, hammer, hat, head, heart, helicopter, hippo, horse, house . . .
- Have students fill the box with things that begin with /h/. Students can write the letter <u>h</u>, draw pictures of things that begin with /h/, cut out and paste up pictures of things that begin with /h/, or write words that begin with /h/.

Note: Neat work helps students take pride in their efforts.

SOLO STORY READING INSTRUCTIONS

Students read from their own storybooks.

COMPREHENSION BUILDING:
DISCUSSION QUESTIONS AND TEACHER THINK ALOUDS

Ask questions and discuss text on the first or second reading, when indicated in the storybook in light gray text.

PROCEDURES

1. First Reading

Have students identify the picture words {whale}, {tail}, {eyes}, and {happy}; then choral read the student text.

2. Second Reading

- Mix group and individual turns, independent of your voice. Have students work toward an accuracy goal of 0–2 errors. Quietly keep track of errors made by all students in each group.
- After reading the story, practice any difficult words.
- If the group has not reached the accuracy goal, have the group reread the story, mixing group and individual turns.

3. Repeated Readings

a. Timed Readings

- Once the accuracy goal has been achieved, have individual students read the page while the other children track the text with their fingers and whisper read.

  Time individuals for 30 seconds and encourage each student to work for his or her personal best.

- Count the number of words read correctly in 30 seconds (words read minus errors).

  Multiply by two to determine words read correctly per minute. Record student scores.

Note: Time students who are confident and enjoy the challenge. If a student is unable to read with close to 100% accuracy, do not time the student. The personal goal should be accuracy. See page 9 for procedures.

b. Partner Reading

During students' daily independent work, have them do Partner Reading.

c. Homework 1

Have students read the story at home. (A reprint of this story is available on a blackline master in *Read Well* Homework.)

STORY 2, SOLO

CHAPTER 2

The

Whales are mammals that live in the sea. These huge animals have a backbone.
They breathe air and take care of their babies.
Some people love to go whale watching.[1]

"Meet the ," said the man.

"See him swim and swim."

"We see him!" said Nan and Dan.

"I see his ," said Nan.

"I see his 2 s," said Dan.

Dan and Nan seem 😃.

What is the whale doing?[2] (Swimming)
Where is he swimming?[3] (In the sea, in the ocean)
Where does the whale live?[4] (The sea, the ocean)
If you went on a boat trip in the sea, what would you want to see?[5]

12

FOCUS ON EXPRESSION
Before the second reading, have students practice two or three sentences at a time. Model and guide expressive reading. Say something like: I think the man was excited when he told the children to meet the whale. Listen to me read the first two sentences . . . Now you try it.
Acknowledge efforts. Listen to [Lindsey] read what Nan said. She can make Nan sound excited.

❶ **Making Connections**

❷ **Identifying—Action**

❸ **Identifying—Where**

❹ **Inferring—Where**

❺ **Making Connections**

13

24

SENTENCE COMPREHENSION

Use work pages from the workbook.

CHECKOUT OPPORTUNITY
Listen to your students read individually while others work.

Multiple Choice Identifying—Who

Multiple Choice Identifying—What

Writing, Complete Sentence

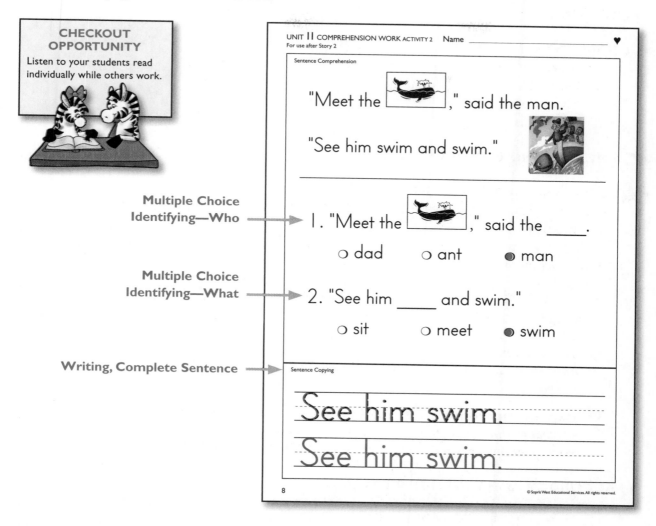

UNIT II COMPREHENSION WORK ACTIVITY 2   Name _____
For use after Story 2

Sentence Comprehension

"Meet the 🐋," said the man.

"See him swim and swim."

1. "Meet the 🐋," said the ____.
   ○ dad   ○ ant   ● man

2. "See him ____ and swim."
   ○ sit   ○ meet   ● swim

Sentence Copying

See him swim.
See him swim.

8

© Sopris West Educational Services. All rights reserved.

PROCEDURES

For each step, demonstrate and guide practice as needed.

1. Sentence Comprehension—Basic Instructions
- Have students read the sentences at the top of the page.
- Have students read items 1 and 2, using the word "blank" when they see the line.
- Have students fill in the circle next to the correct word to fill in the blank.

2. Sentence Tracing and Copying—Basic Instructions
- Have students read and trace the sentence on the first line.
- Have students copy the sentence on the second line.

Note: You may wish to remind students that a sentence begins with a capital letter and ends with a period.

❶ SOUND REVIEW

❷ BEGINNING SOUND

◆◆ **❸ STRETCH AND SHRINK**

cat-caaat-cat	What does a *cat* say? (A *cat* says "meow.")
kid-kiiid-kid	What did the *kid* do? ([She ran home.])
hiss-hiiissss-hiss	What does a mad cat do? (*Hiss*)
hat-haaat-hat	See the cat and the . . . (*hat*).

◆◆ **❹ SMOOTH AND BUMPY BLENDING—CARDS 23, 21**

◆◆ **❺ SOUNDING OUT SMOOTHLY**
- Have students say the underlined part, sound out the word, and then read the word. Use the words in sentences as needed.
- Provide repeated practice, mixing group and individual turns on each word.

Say something like:

Go back to the beginning of the Flower Row. I'm going to count to three while you figure out the first word. Remember, keep the word a secret.

Count quietly, then call on an individual to read the word. Repeat for the remaining words in each row.

✿	*nnneeeed-need*	What do you *need*? (I *need* [help].)
	nnneeeedzzz-needs	[Katie] *needs* [help]. What does [she] need?
	Thththaaat-That	What is *that*? (*That* is a [book].)
♥	*ssseeeemmm-seem*	You *seem* hungry but it's not time for lunch.
	ssseeeemmmzzz-seems	[Thomas] *seems* [happy].
	Sssaaammmzzz-Sam's	That's *Sam's* [dad]. Whose dad is that? (*Sam's*)

❻ ACCURACY AND FLUENCY BUILDING
- Have students say, or sound out, the underlined part of the word, then read the word. Remember, /h/ can be a difficult sound. Have students sound out /Heee/ (as in "He"), /Hiii/ (as in "Him"), and /Haaa/ (as in "Had") before they read the words.
- After students have read the Circle Column, ask them how the words are the same.

❼ TRICKY WORDS
★ **New word: "with"**
Note: "With" is treated as a Tricky Word until Unit 16 due to the unvoiced <u>th</u>.
- Tell students their new word is "with." Have students sound out the word with a soft <u>th</u>.
- Have them read the word five times. Use "with" in sentences.

- Have students silently figure out each word, then read it aloud. Use the words in sentences as needed. Mix group and individual turns, independent of your voice.

❽ DAILY STORY READING
Proceed to the Unit 11 Storybook. See Daily Lesson Planning for pacing suggestions.

❾ COMPREHENSION AND SKILL WORK ACTIVITY 3 AND/OR ACTIVITY 4
See pages 33 and/or 37.

◆◆ For ELLs and children with language delays, provide repeated and extended practice with the language patterns. See page 10 for tips.

UNIT II DECODING PRACTICE 2
(For use with Stories 3 and 4)

1. **SOUND REVIEW** Use Sound Cards for Units 1–11 or Sound Review on Decoding Practice 4.

2. **BEGINNING SOUND** Have students read, trace, and say /h/. Next, have students identify both pictures and then point to the one that begins with /h/.

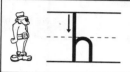 

3. **STRETCH AND SHRINK** Have students orally Stretch and Shrink, then use each word in a sentence.

cat-caaat-cat
kid-kiiid-kid
hiss-hiiissss-hiss
hat-haaat-hat

Do not have students read the words.

4. **SMOOTH AND BUMPY BLENDING** Use Blending Cards 23 and 21.

5. **SOUNDING OUT SMOOTHLY** For each word, have students say the underlined part, sound out the word in one smooth breath, and then read the word.

❀ <u>n</u>eed <u>n</u>eeds Th<u>a</u>t

♥ <u>s</u>eem <u>s</u>eems Sam's

6. **ACCURACY/FLUENCY BUILDING** For each column, have students say the underlined part, then read each word. Next, have students read the column.

✈ <u>H</u>e <u>H</u>im <u>H</u>ad

● <u>and</u> <u>h</u>and <u>s</u>and

★7. **TRICKY WORDS** Introduce "with" using the Tricky Word procedure. Next, have students silently figure out each word, then read it aloud.

▲ as has is his ★with

8. DAILY STORY READING

6

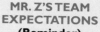 

DUET STORY READING INSTRUCTIONS
Students read from their own storybooks.
The teacher reads the small text and students read the large text.

PACING
- 2- to 4-Day Plans: Have students do the first reading of Duet Story 3.
  Then proceed to repeated readings of Solo Story 4.
- 6- to 10-Day Plans: Have students do the first *and* second readings.

COMPREHENSION BUILDING: DISCUSSION QUESTIONS AND TEACHER THINK ALOUDS
Ask questions and discuss text on the first or second reading when indicated in the storybook in light gray text.

PROCEDURES

1. First Reading

Have students identify the picture word {camel}, then choral read the student text.

2. Second Reading

Have students take turns, with each student reading one line of student text.

More About Mammals

CHAPTER 1
Mammals in Their Habitats

Mammals live in special places called habitats.
What do we call the special places where mammals live?[1] (Habitats)

The giant hippopotamus lives along the rivers of Africa.
Where does the hippo live?[2] (Along the rivers of Africa)

<u>This</u> <u>is</u> <u>his</u> habitat.

<u>He</u> <u>needs</u> to stay wet and cool, so he spends his days in the river.

<u>He</u> <u>has</u> <u>his</u> eyes on top of his head so he can see.

<u>He</u> <u>has</u> <u>his</u> ears on top of his head so he can hear.

<u>He</u> <u>has</u> <u>his</u> nostrils on top of his head so he can breathe.

The hippo is well suited to live along the river where he can spend his days in the water.

14

❶ Defining Vocabulary—Habitats
❷ Identifying—Where

BUILDING COMPREHENSION
Reading and Thinking Aloud (Reminder)

If students have difficulty with a comprehension question, think aloud with them or reread the portion of the story that answers the question. Then, ask the question again.

Look at the picture. Touch the hippo's eyes. Where are they?[1] (On top of his head)
Touch the hippo's ears. Where are they?[2] (On top of his head)
Touch the hippo's nostrils. Where are they?[3] (On top of his head)
Why do you think a hippo has his eyes, ears, and nostrils on top of his head?[4] (So the hippo can see, hear, and breathe—even while he is in the water)

15

❶ Identifying—Where

❷ Identifying—Where

❸ Identifying—Where

❹ Explaining

STORY 3, DUET

Some mammals live in a dry desert habitat. Camels live in the deserts of Africa and Asia. What is the habitat for camels?[1] (The dry desert)

See the man with his .

The man needs the camel to work.

The camel is well suited to his desert life.

He has long eyelashes to keep the sand out of his eyes.

What keeps the sand out of the camel's eyes?[2] (His eyelashes)
We have eyelashes too but they aren't as long. Bat your eyelashes.[3]

He has nostrils he can close to keep the sand out.

Let's pinch our noses. That closes our nostrils.
A camel can close his nostrils to keep out the sand.[4]

He has toes that spread out so he can walk across the sand.

He has a hump on his back. The hump stores food, not water.

Camels can live in the dry desert because they get water from the food they store.
Camels can go for months without food or water. The camel is well suited for his hot, sandy desert habitat.

What is the camel's habitat?[5] (The hot, sandy desert)

16

DECODING ERRORS (Reminder)

If you hear an error, gently correct and have the student reread the sentence.

Have the group practice any difficult words after or between story readings.

INTERVENTION

With low-performing groups, put one or two difficult words on the board and have the whole class practice the words throughout the day.

❶ **Using Vocabulary—Habitat**

❷ **Identifying—What**

❸ **Making Connections**

❹ **Making Connections**

❺ **Using Vocabulary—Habitat**

Touch the camel's eyelashes. What do the long eyelashes do?[1] (Keep the sand out)

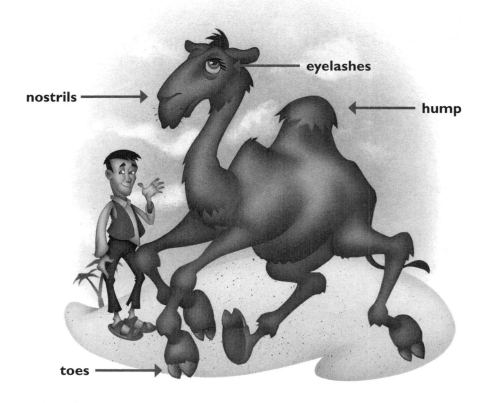

Touch the camel's nostrils. What do they do with their nostrils to keep the sand out of their noses?[2] (They close them.)

Why do the camel's toes spread out when they walk?[3] (It helps the camel walk on the sand.)

Touch the camel's hump. What does the camel store in its hump?[4] (Food)

That's right. Most people think the camel stores water there, but he really stores food.[5]

Camels can be very stubborn and ill-tempered. Some camels even spit at people!

People put up with camels because there aren't any other animals that can carry heavy loads in the desert as well as camels do.

17

[1] **Identifying, Explaining**

[2] **Identifying, Explaining**

[3] **Explaining**

[4] **Identifying—What**

[5] **Teacher Think Aloud**

ALPHABET DETECTIVE
Use work pages from the workbook.

CHECKOUT OPPORTUNITY
Listen to your students read individually while others work.

UNIT II SKILL WORK ACTIVITY 3   Name _____
ALPHABET DETECTIVE: For use after Story 3

H h   ⓘ

H as in Hippo

Capital letter H, small letter h,

H says h.

Happy Hippopotamus,

H, h, h.

© Sopris West Educational Services. All rights reserved.   9

PROCEDURES
For each step, demonstrate and guide practice as needed.

1. Letter Find—Basic Instructions

- Have students look at the first box at the top of the page and follow the directions. Ask:
  What letters will you look for? (The capital letter H and the small letter h)
  What will you do when you find the capital letter H or the small letter h? (Draw a square around it.)

- Have students look at the second box at the top of the page. Ask:
  What other letter will you look for? (The small letter i)
  What will you do when you find the small letter i? (Draw a circle around it.)

- Tell students to follow the directions in the first box for the whole poem; then follow the directions in the second box for the whole poem.

2. Self-Monitoring—Basic Instructions

Have students systematically check each line after finishing the task.

Alternative: At the beginning of the exercise, tell students the number of H's they will draw a square around, and the number of i's they will circle. Have students write the numbers on the top of their paper. When they complete the activity, have them count the number of circles and squares they have drawn. If the numbers are incorrect, they can recheck each line.

3. Coloring—Optional

Have students carefully color the picture, using at least three colors.

Note: If students have difficulty with the multi-step directions, have them do just the first step.

33

SOLO STORY READING INSTRUCTIONS

Students read from their own storybooks.

COMPREHENSION BUILDING:
DISCUSSION QUESTIONS AND TEACHER THINK ALOUDS

Ask questions and discuss text on the first or second reading when indicated in the storybook in light gray text.

PROCEDURES

1. First Reading

Have students identify the picture word {camel}, then choral read the text.

2. Second Reading

- Mix group and individual turns, independent of your voice. Have students work toward an accuracy goal of 0–2 errors. Quietly keep track of errors made by all students in each group.
- After reading the story, practice any difficult words.
- If the group has not reached the accuracy goal, have the group reread the story, mixing group and individual turns.

3. Repeated Readings

a. Timed Readings

- Once the accuracy goal has been achieved, have individual students read the page while the other children track the text with their fingers and whisper read.

  Time individuals for 30 seconds and encourage each student to work for his or her personal best.

- Count the number of words read correctly in 30 seconds (words read minus errors).

  Multiply by two to determine words read correctly per minute. Record student scores.

b. Partner Reading

During students' daily independent work, have them do Partner Reading.

c. Homework 2

Have students read the story at home. (A reprint of this story is available on a blackline master in *Read Well* Homework.)

CHAPTER 2

The Sat

What is this chapter about?[1] (The camel)
What do you already know about camels?[2]

That sat in the sand.

The man said, "I need the .

He seems mad."

The said, "See me sit in the sand."

He said, "See me sit with the sad man."

INDIVIDUAL TURNS
(Reminder)

During individual turns, have all students continue to track text. Students can whisper read during another student's turn to read aloud.

ACKNOWLEDGING DESIRED BEHAVIORS
(Reminder)

Make a special effort to notice the least mature students when they are taking steps towards greater responsibility. Say something like:
[Norton], you were tracking every word that [Zadie] read. It's your turn to read next.

18

❶ Identifying—Topic
❷ Priming Background Knowledge

What do you think the man wants the camel to help him do?[1] (Carry a heavy load)
Why is the man sad?[2] (The camel doesn't want to go.)

❶ **Inferring**
❷ **Inferring**

SENTENCE ILLUSTRATION

Use work pages from the workbook.

Using Vocabulary—Camel
Identifying—What, Who

Writing
Identifying—Where

UNIT II COMPREHENSION WORK ACTIVITY 4   Name _____
For use after Story 4

Sentence Illustration

See the [camel] with the man.

Sentence Completion

The [camel] was in the sand.

The [camel] was
in the sand.

10   © Sopris West Educational Services. All rights reserved.

CHECKOUT OPPORTUNITY

Listen to your students read individually while others work.

PROCEDURES

For each step, demonstrate and guide practice as needed.

1. Sentence Illustration—Specific Instructions
- Have students read the sentence.
- Have students draw a picture of the camel and the man.

2. Sentence Completion—Specific Instructions
- Have students read the sentence.
- Have students identify the part of the sentence that they will complete.
- Have students trace and complete the sentence on the lines provided.

Note: Remind students that a sentence begins with a capital letter and ends with a period.

❶ SOUND REVIEW

Use Sound Cards for Units 1–11 or the Sound Review on Decoding Practice 4.

❷ NEW SOUND PRACTICE

Remember, Theo Bear provides a reference for the lines—hat line, belt line, and shoe line.

◆◆ ❸ STRETCH AND SHRINK

hasn't-haaazzznnnt-hasn't	The [hippo] *hasn't* had lunch. Has [he] had lunch? (No)
didn't-diiidnnnt-didn't	The [dog] *didn't* [bark]. Did [he] bark? (No)
sweet-ssswwweeeet-sweet	This apple tastes good. It is *sweet* and juicy.
swims-ssswwwiiimmmzzz-swims	The [hippo] *swims* in the [river].

◆◆ ❹ SMOOTH AND BUMPY BLENDING—CARDS 23, 19

◆◆ ❺ SOUNDING OUT SMOOTHLY

- Have students say the underlined part, sound out the word, and then read the word. Use the words in sentences as needed.
- Repeat practice. Mix group and individual turns, independent of your voice.

✿ *ssswwwiiimmm-swim*	What do you do in a swimming pool? (*Swim*)
ssswwwiiimmmzzz-swims	The [hippo] *swims* in the [river].
Daaadzzz-Dad's	That's *Dad's* [car]. Whose [car] is that? (*Dad's*)

❻ ACCURACY AND FLUENCY BUILDING

- For each column, have students say the underlined part, then read each word.
- Have students read the whole column.
- Repeat practice on each column, building accuracy first and then fluency.

❼ TRICKY WORDS

Provide plenty of practice on the Tricky Words. By the end of Unit 11, students should know: "I," "I'm," "said," "the," "was," "The," "is," "his," "as," "has," and "with."

TRICKY WORD PRACTICE

Whole Class Practice

On the board, write a list of Tricky Words that are easy for the lowest performing student in your class. Add one difficult word with a star by it.

Practice the list with the whole class—as a part of your morning opening, before going to lunch, after coming in from recess, and before going home.

INDIVIDUAL PRACTICE

Write one difficult word on a sticky note. Place the child's *special* word on his or her desk. Several times throughout the day, have the child read the word and use it in a sentence. Let the child take his or her special sticky note home at the end of the day.

---

❽ DAILY STORY READING

Proceed to the Unit 11 Storybook. See Daily Lesson Planning for pacing suggestions.

❾ COMPREHENSION AND SKILL WORK ACTIVITY 5 AND/OR ACTIVITY 6

See pages 45 and/or 51.

◆◆ For ELLs and children with language delays, provide repeated and extended practice with the language patterns. See page 10 for tips.

UNIT 11 DECODING PRACTICE 3
(For use with Stories 5 and 6)

1. SOUND REVIEW Use Sound Cards for Units 1–11 or Sound Review on Decoding Practice 4.

2. NEW SOUND PRACTICE Have students read the sound, then trace and say it.

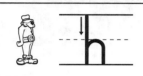 

3. STRETCH AND SHRINK Have students orally Stretch and Shrink, then use each word in a sentence.

hasn't-haaazzznnnt-hasn't
didn't-diiidnnnt-didn't
sweet-ssswwweeeet-sweet
swims-ssswwwiiimmmzzz-swims

Do not have students read the words.

4. SMOOTH AND BUMPY BLENDING Use Blending Cards 23 and 19.

5. SOUNDING OUT SMOOTHLY For each word, have students say the underlined part, sound out the word in one smooth breath, and then read the word.

❀ sw**i**m   **swims**   D**a**d's

6. ACCURACY/FLUENCY BUILDING For each column, have students say the underlined part, then read each word. Next, have students read the column.

☆	✈	●
h**i**d	**a**t	m**ee**t
h**a**d	h**a**t	m**a**t
h**e**	s**a**t	m**i**tt
		mi**nt**

7. TRICKY WORDS Have students silently figure out each word and then read it aloud.

▲ H**i**s w**a**s w**i**th h**a**s **i**s

8. DAILY STORY READING

7

DUET STORY READING INSTRUCTIONS

Students read from their own storybooks.

The teacher reads the small text and students read the large text.

PACING

- 3- to 4-Day Plans: Have students do the first reading of Duet Story 5.

  Then proceed to repeated readings of Solo Story 6.

- 6- to 10-Day Plans: Have students do the first *and* second readings.

COMPREHENSION BUILDING: DISCUSSION QUESTIONS AND TEACHER THINK ALOUDS

Ask questions and discuss text on the first or second reading when indicated in the storybook in light gray text.

PROCEDURES

1. First Reading

- Tell students they are going to read the next chapter about a hippo named Sam.
- Have students choral read the student text.

2. Second Reading

Have students take turns, with each student reading one line of student text.

ECHO READING
(Reminder)
Periodically, repeat the text with good expression and phrasing to enhance meaning.

STORY 5, DUET

CHAPTER 3

A Hippo Named Sam

What do you think this story will be about?[1] (A hippo named Sam)
Hippos are mammals. Listen carefully for facts that tell Sam is a mammal.[2]

Hippos are huge and interesting mammals. They live in the rivers of Africa. We call this their habitat—the special place they live on earth.
What is a habitat?[3] (The special place an animal lives. A hippo lives in the rivers of Africa.)

This is Sam and his mother.

Sam was just born, but he can already swim.

He swims with his mother.

He swims in the river.

Sam has fun in his river habitat.

Who is Sam?[4] (Sam is a baby hippo.)
What can a baby hippo do?[5] (Swim)
Who is Sam swimming with?[6] (His mother)
Do you think Sam is a mammal?[7] (Yes)
What fact makes you think he is a mammal?[8] (His mother is taking care of him.)

20

❶ **Predicting**

❷ **Priming Background Knowledge**

❸ **Defining Vocabulary—Habitat**

❹ **Identifying—Who**

❺ **Identifying—Action**

❻ **Identifying—Who**

❼ **Classifying**

❽ **Applying**

Sam has two nostrils on the top of his head so he can breathe air while the rest of his body is under the water.

Sam has eyes on top of his head so he can see,

and he has ears on top of his head so he can hear.

Touch Sam's nostrils. Can he breathe air while he's in the water?[1] (Yes)
How?[2] (He breathes through the nostrils on top of his head.)
Touch Sam's eyes. Can he see while he's in the water?[3] (Yes)
Touch Sam's ears. Can he hear while he's in the water?[4] (Yes)
I think Sam is well suited for his river habitat.[5]

21

❶ **Identifying, Affirming**

❷ **Explaining**

❸ **Identifying, Affirming**

❹ **Identifying, Affirming**

❺ **Teacher Think Aloud**

<u>See</u> <u>Sam</u> <u>and</u> <u>his</u> herd.

The herd stays in the water during the hot day.

22

At night, the herd walks on the riverbank looking for food.

Sam's dad is the leader of the herd.

See Sam with his dad.

His dad is huge. He weighs as much as two cars.

How big is Sam's dad?[1] (He is huge. He weighs as much as two cars.)
Do you think Sam will weigh that much someday?[2]

When Sam is grown, he will eat 130 pounds of grass, leaves, and fruit each day.
What do hippos eat?[3] (Grass, leaves, and fruit) How much do they eat?[4] (A lot)
Perhaps one day, Sam will be the leader of his herd.

23

❶ Describing
❷ Predicting
❸ Identifying—What
❹ Describing

SKILL WORK ACTIVITY 5

HEARING SOUNDS

Use work pages from the workbook.

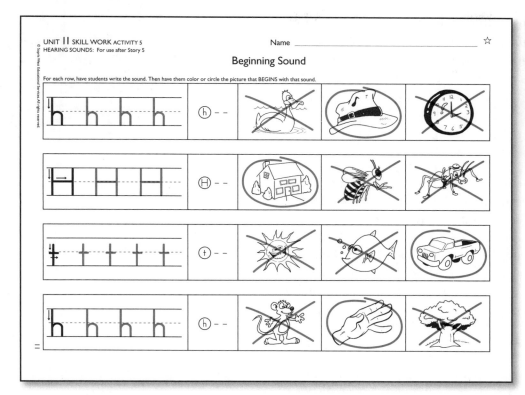

CHECKOUT OPPORTUNITY

Listen to your students read individually while others work.

PICTURE WORDS (Reminder)

Make sure that students know which sound they are looking for (beginning) and that they can identify the picture words prior to working independently.

ANSWERS

Line 1: duck, <u>hat</u>, clock
Line 2: <u>house</u>, bee, ant
Line 3: sun, fish, <u>truck</u>
Line 4: mouse, <u>hand</u>, tree

PROCEDURES

Beginning Sound

Demonstrate and guide practice as needed.

• Have students write the beginning sound on the line.
• Have students color the picture word that begins with that sound.

Alternative: Have students write the beginning sound on the line, circle the picture word that begins with the sound, and cross out the picture words that do not begin with the sound.

45

SOLO STORY READING INSTRUCTIONS

Students read from their own storybooks.

COMPREHENSION BUILDING:
DISCUSSION QUESTIONS AND TEACHER THINK ALOUDS

Ask questions and discuss text on the first or second reading when indicated in the storybook in light gray text.

PROCEDURES

1. First Reading

Have students choral read the text.

2. Second Reading

- Mix group and individual turns, independent of your voice.
  Have students work toward an accuracy goal of 0–2 errors.
  Quietly keep track of errors made by all students in each group.
- After reading the story, practice any difficult words.
- If the group has not reached the accuracy goal, have the group reread the story, mixing group and individual turns.

3. Repeated Readings

a. Timed Readings

- Once the accuracy goal has been achieved, have individual students read the page while the other children track the text with their fingers and whisper read.
  Time individuals for 30 seconds and encourage each student to work for his or her personal best.
- Count the number of words read correctly in 30 seconds (words read minus errors).
  Multiply by two to determine words read correctly per minute.
  Record student scores.

b. Partner Reading

During students' daily independent work, have them do Partner Reading.

c. Homework 3

Have students read the story at home. (A reprint of this story is available on a blackline master in *Read Well* Homework.)

STORY 6, SOLO

CHAPTER 4
With His Dad

What is the title of this chapter?[1] ("With His Dad")

This is Sam.

He swims and swims.

Sam sees his dad.

He needs his dad.

Who is the story about?[2] (Sam)
What is Sam?[3] (A baby hippo)
Who does Sam need?[4] (His dad)
Sam is a mammal. Baby mammals spend a lot of time with their parents.[5]

24

❶ Identifying—Title

❷ Identifying—Who

❸ Identifying—What

❹ Identifying—Who

❺ Teacher Think Aloud

This is Sam's dad.

Sam swims with his dad.

He and his dad swim and swim.

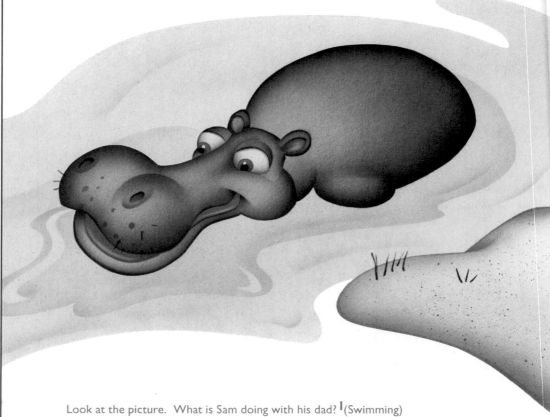

Look at the picture. What is Sam doing with his dad? [1](Swimming)
Why would Sam swim with his dad? [2](He is a mammal. Mammals stay with their parents . . .)

25

❶ Identifying—Action
❷ Inferring, Applying

★ **COMPREHENSION BUILDING: FACT SUMMARY**

Read the text and have students identify whether animals are mammals
or not as indicated by the procedures in light gray text. Children's
mastery of facts is the food for higher order thinking. In this Fact
Summary students conclude with an inductive thinking exercise.

Facts About Mammals[1]

Let's review some of the facts we learned about mammals.

Fact one:
Mammals have a . . . backbone.
Touch the backbone of the cat.

Fact two:
Mammals breathe . . . air.

Fact three:
Mammals have . . . fur or hair.

Fact four:
Mammals take care of their . . . babies.

Let's make a list of animals we think are mammals.[2]
Now we can ask ourselves questions to see if they are really mammals.[3]

Do [dogs] have a backbone?
Do [dogs] breathe air?
Do [dogs] have hair or fur?
Do [dogs] take care of their babies after they are born?

26

❶ **Building Knowledge, Summarizing**

❷ **Applying**

❸ **Classifying**

Research Snapshot

CONTENT KNOWLEDGE

Results of the National Assessment of Educational Progress have consistently shown that children of poverty score significantly lower than more advantaged children. With the documentation of a "fourth-grade slump" in achievement (Chall, Jacobs, & Baldwin, 1990), multiple researchers and policy writers (Adams, 1990; Hart & Risley, 1995; Snow, Burns, & Griffin, 1998; Stanovich, 1986) are advocating instruction that includes early instruction and immersion in language, vocabulary, and content knowledge.

From the earliest ages, reading is much more than decoding. From the start, reading is also accessing and further acquiring language knowledge and domain knowledge. This means that instruction and practice in fluency of decoding needs to be accompanied by instruction and practice in vocabulary and domain knowledge. If we want to raise later achievement and avoid the fourth-grade slump we need to combine early instruction in the procedures of literacy with early instruction in the content of literacy, specifically: vocabulary, conventions of language, and knowledge of the world (Chall and Jacobs, 2003, p.21).

In addition to explicit instruction in word recognition and fluency, *Read Well* systematically builds content knowledge, language, and vocabulary through topics such as snakes and caterpillars, Harriet Tubman and Martin Luther King, metamorphosis, and the classification of animals.

The interwoven nature of related topics and activities across the program allows the incremental building of vocabulary and specific content knowledge. As recommended by research, knowledge is built recursively through (a) listening comprehension during *Read Well*'s unique duet text format, (b) oral language activities (e.g., discussion questions and oral summaries), and (c) student-read text and written activities (illustration, multiple choice, graphic organizers and summarization).

RHYMING PATTERNS

Use work pages from the workbook.

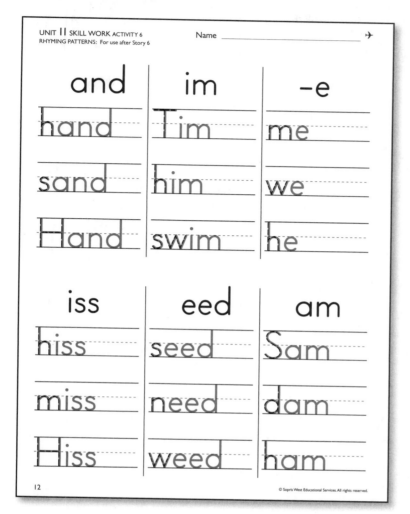

UNIT II SKILL WORK ACTIVITY 6
RHYMING PATTERNS: For use after Story 6

Name _____

and	im	-e
hand	Tim	me
sand	him	we
Hand	swim	he

iss	eed	am
hiss	seed	Sam
miss	need	dam
Hiss	weed	ham

12

PROCEDURES

Rhyming Patterns—Basic Instructions

- For each box, have students read the pattern at the top and then trace the letters and write the pattern on the lines to make words.
- Remind students to read the pattern words to themselves or to a partner when they finish the exercise.

Note: There are multiple uses for Decoding Practice 4.
- Use the Sound Review rows in place of Sound Card Practice.
- Use the whole page at the end of the unit for fluency building and/or to informally assess skills.
- Have students complete the page as a partner review.
- Build spelling dictation lessons from the sounds and words on this page.

❶ SOUND REVIEW

★ ❷ ACCURACY AND FLUENCY BUILDING

Purpose
The Accuracy and Fluency Building exercises on this page provide an additional opportunity for students to build automatic recognition of word families, generalize patterns to new words, and learn to carefully discriminate the letter changes in words that change meaning.

✈ Columns
Use the Airplane Columns to build fluency. Once students can read a column accurately, model a pace that is slightly faster than the students' current response rate. Then have students read the column at that rate.

✿ Columns
The Flower Columns provide practice in making fine discriminations among words. Focus students' attention on careful, accurate reading, and remind them that even slight changes affect word meaning.

❸ TRICKY WORDS
Remember, students have just learned five new Tricky Words. Have students practice these rows until they can read all the words with 100% accuracy. Then, have them practice the words to build their response rate.

❹ DAILY STORY READING
See Daily Lesson Planning for story suggestions.

SOUNDING OUT WITH /H/

Sounding out with the /h/ sound is the hardest blending task.

Provide extra whole class practice orally blending words that begin with /h/. Use the following patterning:

ha-haaat (hat)

hi-hiiit (hit)

he-heaeaeat (heat)

Write the following words on the chalkboard and have students read one or two words periodically throughout the day.

ham (ha-ham)

him (hi-him)

had (ha-had)

hat (ha-hat)

UNIT 11 DECODING PRACTICE 4
(See Daily Lesson Planning for story suggestions.)

1. SOUND REVIEW Demonstrate an appropriate pace. Have students read the sounds in each row.

■	W	ee	s	w	t	a	6
✿	th	n	d	A	w	T	12
♥	e	W	m	t	ee	w	18
●	N	a	th	e	w	D	24

★ 2. ACCURACY/FLUENCY BUILDING For each column, have students say the underlined part, then read each word. Next, have students read the column. See the Teacher's Guide for important information.

✈	✈✈	✈✈✈	✿	✿✿
h<u>im</u>	s<u>a</u>t	w<u>e</u>	H<u>i</u>d	<u>Th</u>e
sw<u>im</u>	m<u>a</u>t	h<u>e</u>	H<u>a</u>d	<u>Th</u>an
T<u>im</u>	th<u>a</u>t	m<u>e</u>	H<u>ee</u>d	<u>Th</u>is
d<u>im</u>	h<u>a</u>t	D<u>ee</u>	W<u>ee</u>d	<u>Th</u>at

3. TRICKY WORDS Have students silently figure out each word and then read it aloud.

☆☆	his	The	as	I'm	was
☆☆	said	is	has	with	is

4. DAILY STORY READING

8

RHYTHMIC PRACTICE

Students enjoy variety. Practice Accuracy and Fluency Columns by periodically practicing with a rhythm of your choice. Say something like:

Listen to me do the first Airplane Column with this rhythm.

-im, -im, him

-im, -im, swim

Try the next words with me.

-im, -im, Tim

-im, -im, dim

Now try it by yourself with the first Flower Column.

53

End of the Unit

In this section, you will find:

Making Decisions

As you near the end of the unit, you will need to make decisions. Should you administer the Decoding Assessment or should you teach Extra Practice lessons?

Unit 11 Decoding Assessment

The Unit 11 Decoding Assessment is located on page 56 and can also be found in the *Assessment Manual*.

Certificate of Achievement and Goal Setting

Celebrate your children's accomplishments.

Extra Practice

Lessons and blackline masters for added decoding practice and independent work are provided for students who need extended practice opportunities.

Making Decisions

ASSESSMENT READINESS

Assess when students are able to easily complete decoding tasks from the beginning of a lesson.

- If you aren't sure whether students are ready for the assessment, give the assessment. Do Extra Practice lessons if needed.
- If students are not ready for the assessment, proceed to the Extra Practice lessons. Administer the assessment as soon as students are ready.

GENERAL ASSESSMENT GUIDELINES

Assess all students.

- Assess each child individually.
- Score student responses on the Student Assessment Record, adhering to the scoring criteria in the *Assessment Manual*. Use a stopwatch to time how long it takes the student to read Subtest D.
- Follow the general instructions at the bottom of each assessment. Record a Strong Pass, a Weak Pass, or a No Pass.

> **SPECIAL SCORING INFORMATION**
>
> **Sounding Out Smoothly**
>
> If a student reads the word without sounding out in Subtest B, give the student positive feedback, but check to see that the student can sound out the word.
>
> Say something like:
> You can read the word very easily. Now I'd like to see if you can sound it out slowly and smoothly—really stretch that word out.

ACCELERATION

- If students score 100% across all subtests and read Subtest D in less than 30 seconds, consider shortening units. Do not skip Unit 12.
- If an individual student scores 100% across all subtests and reads Subtest D significantly faster than other students in the group, assess the student for placement in the next higher group.

INTERVENTION OPTIONS—INDIVIDUALS

1. Add informal practice throughout the day.
2. Add practice with repeated readings on Solo Stories, Homework and Extra Practice. See page 9 for specific information
3. Find ways to provide a double dose of *Read Well* instruction.
   Have an instructional assistant provide instruction with Extra Practice lessons.
4. Consider placement in a lower group.

INTERVENTION OPTIONS—GROUP

1. Extend the unit with Extra Practice lessons.
2. Consider a Jell-Well Review before moving forward. (See the *Assessment Manual*.)

CERTIFICATE OF ACHIEVEMENT AND GOAL SETTING

When students pass the assessment, celebrate with the Certificate of Achievement. Then, set a personal goal. (See *Getting Started*.)

SUBTEST A. SOUNDS   GOAL 6/7

h	i	W	ee	d	H	a

SUBTEST B. SOUNDING OUT SMOOTHLY   GOAL 4/5

than	had	we	Sam's	swim

SUBTEST C. TRICKY WORDS   GOAL 3/4

as	The	His	was

SUBTEST D. SENTENCES   Desired Fluency: 30 seconds or less (30 wcpm)   GOAL 13/15

He said, "That man is mad."

Nat has seeds.

Sam's hat was in the sand.

SCORING   If the student needs assistance, the item is incorrect.
STRONG PASS   The student meets the goals on all subtests and has attained the desired fluency. Proceed to Unit 12.
WEAK PASS   The student meets the goals on 3 out of 4 subtests and/or fails to attain the desired fluency. Proceed to Unit 12 with added practice, or provide Extra Practice lessons in Unit 11, and/or provide a Jell-Well Review.
NO PASS   The student fails to meet the goal on 2 or more subtests. Provide Extra Practice lessons and retest, and/or provide a Jell-Well Review.

Certificate of Achievement

This certifies that

_____ ,

on this _____ day of _____ , _____ ,

has successfully completed

Read Well Unit 11

Sounds Mastered: s, e, ee, m, a, d, th, n, t, w, i, Th, h

Words Mastered: I, see, I'm, me, am, Sam, mam, seem, sad, seed, mad, add, dad, said, seeds, seems, the, Nan, man, sees, Sams, an, and, than, Dan, seen, deed, sand, need, Dan, needs, at, sat, meet, meets, that, mat, ant, ants, was, Ann, we, weed, weeds, sweet, Nat, Dee, tan, in, it, sit, this, did, Tim, wind, that's, miss, win, mist, mints, tin, teen, sits, as, has, is, his, with, Dad's, dim, had, hand, hat, he, heed, hid, him, mint, mitt, Sam's, swim, swims

Personal Goal Setting

I would like to be able to:

_____

I can work on my goal by:

_____

My teacher will tell me when he or she notices me working on my goal.

Date _____   Student Signature _____

Teacher Signature _____

❶ SMOOTH AND BUMPY BLENDING

Select from Blending Cards 1–23 for review.

❷ STRETCH AND SHRINK

he-heee-he   Look at [Julian]. What is *he* doing? (*He* is [reading].)
had-haaad-had   Yesterday, we *had* . . . [fun].
him-hiiimmm-him Look at [Dillon]. See *him* [read].

❸ SOUND DICTATION

Have students write each sound, then check and correct.

/h/ at the beginning of "hippo" with small letter <u>h</u>
/iii/ at the beginning of "insect" with small letter <u>i</u>
/www/ at the beginning of "wind" with small letter <u>w</u>

> **CAUTION**
> Your children may not need Extra Practice. If in doubt, assess students and include Extra Practice only if needed.

❹ WORD DICTATION

Have students count the sounds in each word with their fingers, identify and write each sound, and then read the word.

he   Look at [Julian]. What is *he* doing? (*He* is [reading].)
had   Yesterday, we *had* . . . [fun].
him   Look at [Dillon]. See *him* [read].

The first word is "he." Look at [Julian]. What is *he* doing? (*He* is [reading].)
We're going to count the sounds in "he."
Tell me the first sound. **Hold up one finger.** (/h/)
Tell me the next sound. **Hold up two fingers**. (/eee/)
How many sounds are in "he"? (Two)

Tell me the first sound. (/h/) Write it.
Tell me the next sound. (/eee/) Write it.
Do Smooth Blending. (/heee/) Read the word. (he)
Look at [Julian]. What is *he* doing? (*He* is [reading].)
Repeat with "had" and "him."

> **DICTATION**
> • Demonstrate and guide practice as needed.
> • Have students check and correct.

❺ POSSESSIVE '<u>S</u>

• Have students sound out each word, then read the phrase.
• Repeat practice, mixing group and individual turns, independent of your voice.

❻ SOUNDING OUT SMOOTHLY

Have students sound out the word, then read the word.

❼ TRICKY WORDS

Repeat practice, mixing group and individual turns, independent of your voice.

❽ DAILY STORY READING

Proceed to Extra Practice Activity 1.
• Have students read each sentence from the book.
• Repeat, mixing group and individual turns, independent of your voice.

❾ EXTRA PRACTICE ACTIVITY I—CHECKOUT OPPORTUNITY

Have students fold, color, and read the book.

◆◆ For ELLs and children with language delays, provide repeated and extended practice with the language patterns. See page 10 for tips.

Name _____

1. SMOOTH AND BUMPY BLENDING Select from Blending Cards 1–23 for review.

2. STRETCH AND SHRINK Have students orally
Stretch and Shrink, then use each word in a sentence..

3. SOUND DICTATION Have students write each sound, then check and correct:
/h/ at the beginning of "hippo," /iii/ at the beginning of "insect," /www/ at the beginning of "wind."

he-heee-he
had-haaad-had
him-hiiimmm-him

Do not have students read the words.

_____   _____   _____

- - - - - - - -   - - - - - - - -   - - - - - - - -

_____   _____   _____

4. WORD DICTATION Have students count the sounds in each word, identify and write each sound, and then read the word: "he," "had," and "him."

_____   _____   _____

- - - - - - - -   - - - - - - - -   - - - - - - - -

1 _____   2 _____   3 _____

5. POSSESSIVE 'S Have students sound out each word, then read the phrase.

 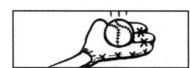 

| Sam's hat | Nat's mitt | Dad's mint |

6. SOUNDING OUT SMOOTHLY For each word, have students sound out the word in one smooth breath, and then read the word.

| ❁ man | had | seeds | This |
| ❁❁ swim | than | sands | That |

7. TRICKY WORDS For each word, have students silently figure out the word, then read it aloud.

| His | with | as | is | has |

8. DAILY STORY READING

Who Is the Mammal in the Hat?

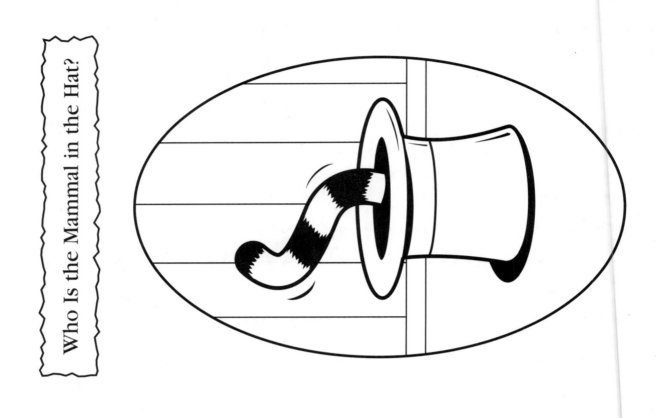

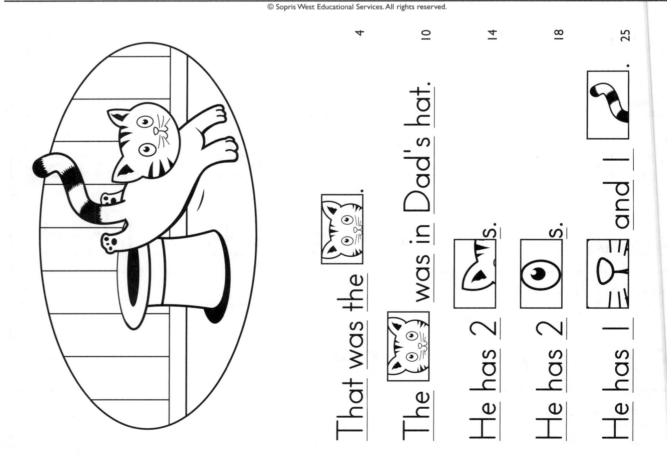

That was the .   4

The was in Dad's hat.   10

He has 2 s.   14

He has 2 s.   18

He has 1 and 1 .   25

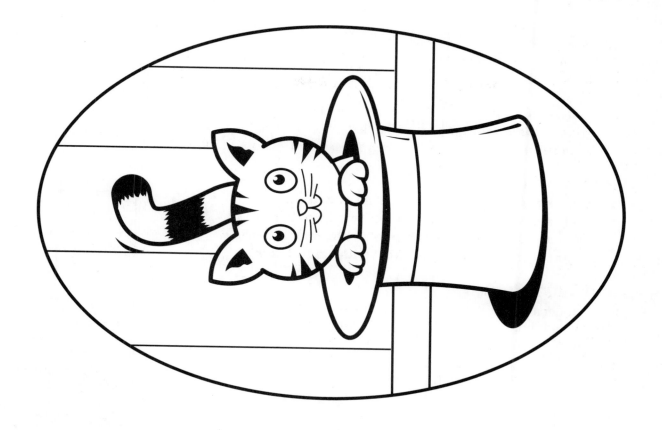

4

8

12

16

21

27

He has 2 s.

He has 2 _____s.

He has 1 _____.

He has 1 _____.

He is in Dad's hat.

See him sit in that hat.

◆◆ ❶ SMOOTH AND BUMPY BLENDING

Select from Blending Cards 1–23 for review.

◆◆ ❷ STRETCH AND SHRINK

hat-haaat-hat	See the cat and the . . . (*hat*).
that-thththaaat-that	What is *that*? (*That* is a [pencil].)
Nat's-Nnnaaatsss-Nat's	That's *Nat's* [desk]. Whose [desk] is that? (*Nat's*)

❸ SOUND DICTATION

Have students write each sound, then check and correct.

/iii/ at the beginning of "insect" with small letter i

/h/ at the beginning of "hippo" with small letter h

/aaa/ at the beginning of "ant" with small letter a

> **CAUTION**
>
> Your children may not need Extra Practice. If in doubt, assess students and include Extra Practice only if needed.

> **HAVE STUDENTS CHECK AND CORRECT.**

◆◆ ❹ WORD DICTATION

Have students count the sounds in each word with their fingers, identify and write each sound, and then read the word.

hat	See the cat and the . . . (*hat*).
that	What is *that*? (*That* is a [pencil].)
Nat's	That's *Nat's* [desk]. Whose [desk] is that? (*Nat's*)

The first word is "hat." See the cat and the . . . (*hat*).
We're going to count the sounds in "hat."
Tell me the first sound. **Hold up one finger.** (/h/)
Repeat with /aaa/ and /t/.
How many sounds are in "hat"? (Three)

Tell me the first sound. (/h/) Write it.
Repeat with /aaa/ and /t/.
Do Smooth Blending. (/haaat/) Read the word. (hat)
See the cat and the . . . (hat).
Repeat with "that" and "Nat's."

❺ ACCURACY/FLUENCY BUILDING

• For each column, have students say the underlined part, then read the word.
• Have students read the whole column.
• Repeat practice on each column, building accuracy first and then fluency.

❻ TRICKY WORDS

Repeat practice, mixing group and individual turns, independent of your voice.

❼ DAILY STORY READING

Proceed to Extra Practice Activity 2.
• Have students read each sentence.
• Repeat, mixing group and individual turns, independent of your voice.

❽ EXTRA PRACTICE ACTIVITY 2—CHECKOUT OPPORTUNITY

As you listen to individuals read the story, have students color the picture.

Name_____

1. SMOOTH AND BUMPY BLENDING Select from Blending Cards 1–23 for review.

2. STRETCH AND SHRINK Have students orally Stretch and Shrink, then use each word in a sentence.

hat-haaat-hat
that-thththaaat-that
Nat's-Nnnaaatsss-Nat's

Do not have students read the words.

3. SOUND DICTATION Have students write each sound, then check and correct: /iii/ at the beginning of "insect," /h/ at the beginning of "hippo," /aaa/ at the beginning of "ant."

_____   _____   _____

4. WORD DICTATION Have students count the sounds in each word, identify and write each sound, and then read the word: "hat," "that," and "Nat's."

1 _____   2 _____   3 _____

5. ACCURACY/FLUENCY BUILDING In each column, have students say the underlined part, then read each word. Next, have students read the column.

♥	♥♥	♥♥♥
h̲e	sw<u>im</u>	m<u>a</u>t
h̲id	T<u>im</u>	m<u>i</u>tt
h̲ad	h<u>im</u>	m<u>i</u>st
h̲and	h<u>i</u>t	m<u>ee</u>t
h̲am	s<u>i</u>t	m<u>i</u>nt

6. TRICKY WORDS For each word, have students silently figure out the word, then read it aloud.

with   The   has   said   was

7. DAILY STORY READING

Name_____

Matt the

This is Matt.   3

He is an .   7

See his s and his s.   13

See his .   16

Matt needs weeds.   19

Matt seems sad.   22

My goal is to read with 0–2 errors. This is what I did:

Have students read the sentences. Time individual students for 30 seconds; mark errors. To determine words correct per minute (wcpm), count words read in 30 seconds, subtract errors, multiply times two, and record on the chart. If student completes the passage in less than 30 seconds, have him or her return to the top and continue reading. (Repeated readings may be completed with older students, assistants, or parents.)

Reading	1st	2nd	3rd	4th
Errors				
Words/ 30 seconds				
wcpm				

① STORYBOOK DECODING REVIEW

For each row, mix group and individual turns, independent of your voice.

② SOLO STORY REVIEW— UNITS 8 AND 9

- Guide student reading, gradually increasing rate.
- Mix group and individual turns on the stories, independent of your voice.
- Repeat practice. While one student reads, have others track the text with their fingers and whisper read.

③ EXTRA PRACTICE ACTIVITY 3—CHECKOUT OPPORTUNITY

- Have students cut out the Letter Cards and arrange them on the Letter Card Grid to create the words "had," "him," "hat," "hid," "he," "That," and "This" in the blank row at the top of the page.
- Have students arrange and glue the letters in the remaining rows to create "hat, "had," and "him." (While students are gluing, listen to individuals read a Solo Story.)

Challenge Activity: With the remaining letters, have students make a word in the blank row.

> **CAUTION**
>
> Your children may not need Extra Practice 3 and 4. If in doubt, assess students and include Extra Practice only if needed.

① DECODING PRACTICE 4 REVIEW

For each row, mix group and individual turns, independent of your voice.

② SOLO STORY REVIEW—UNITS 10 AND 11

- Guide student reading, gradually increasing rate and emphasizing expression.
- Mix group and individual turns on the stories, independent of your voice.
- Repeat practice. While one student reads, have others track the text with their fingers and whisper read.

③ EXTRA PRACTICE ACTIVITY 4—CHECKOUT OPPORTUNITY

- Have students cut out the Memory Cards. (While students are cutting out their cards, listen to individuals read a Solo Story.)
- Once the cards have been cut out, have the group or pairs of students play Memory.

  Using one set of cards, spread the cards out in rows with the words facing down.

  Have students take turns. Each time a card is turned over, have the group or pair identify the word.

  If the words match, have students set the pair off to the side.

  If the words do not match, have students turn the cards back over and try again.

h	h	h
a	a	e
i	d	m
t	Th	s

Name_____

Letter Card Grid

	a	t
h	a	
h	i	

has	him	That
has	him	That
is	man	with
is	man	with
the	Nat	Nat

Note: The Memory Cards can also be used to create sentences. Also, please note there is no match for the word "the."